BLOODLINES

BLOODLINES

Odyssey of a Native Daughter

JANET CAMPBELL HALE

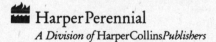

HarperPerennial

A Division of HarperCollins*Publishers*

A hardcover edition of this book was published in 1993 by Random House, Inc. It is here reprinted by arrangement with Random House, Inc.

HarperCollins books may be purchased for educational, business, or sales promotional use. For information please write: Special Markets Department, HarperCollins Publishers, Inc., 10 East 53rd Street, New York, NY 10022.

First HarperPerennial edition published 1994.

Designed by Gloria Tso

Library of Congress Cataloging-in-Publication Data
Hale, Janet Campbell.
    Bloodlines : odyssey of a native daughter / Janet Campbell Hale. —
1st HarperPerennial ed.
        p.   cm.
        ISBN 0-06-097612-8
        1. Hale, Janet Campbell.   2. Skitswish women—Biography.
    3. Skitswish Indians—Social life and customs.
[E99.S63H35   1994]
818'.5403—dc20
[B]   94-3999

94 95 96 97 98 RRD/VA 10 9 8 7 6 5 4 3 2 1

For All My Relations

"The guts of any significant fiction—or autobiography—is an anguished question."

—WALLACE STEGNER
"The Law of Nature and the Dream of Man"

Acknowledgments

Thanks to: *My husband, Muhammad Ashraf,*
my friends, Roberta Wilson, Juanita Jefferson and
Donna Langston,
my editor at Random House, Jennifer Ash.

Thank you all very much for the vital support you have given me and my work. It was much needed and is much appreciated.

Thanks to the D'arcy McNickle Center for the Study of the History of the American Indian at the Newberry Library in Chicago, Illinois, for the fellowship that permitted me to do research on the McLoughlin family and the fur-trade era in North America.

Thanks to John Aubrey of the McNickle Center for doing research for me verifying the little-known incident in 1877 that drew thirty Cocur d'Alene tribal members into the Nez Percé Conflict.

Contents

Circling Raven:
An Introduction

One day in the year 1740, the story goes, a raven, circling in the sky above a Coeur d'Alene village, spoke to the head chief.

"Did you understand?" the chief (who would henceforth be known as Chief Circling Raven) asked the others. No one understood but he. This is what the raven told him:

"A great evil is coming. An enemy more powerful than any you have ever known will surround you. Even now your enemy has spied you. There will be much bloodshed. Much sorrow. Gather your strength. Before the enemy three ravens will come to you. Their teachings will help you survive the coming onslaught."

That is how it happened that the arrival of three Black Robes (Jesuit missionaries) in the mid 1800s was regarded as the fulfillment of a prophecy and the Coeur d'Alene people converted to Catholicism. By then everyone knew who the terrible enemy was.

The Coeur d'Alene tribe has been through a lot of changes since their conversion one hundred and fifty years ago. A terrible enemy did come, just as the circling raven foretold, and made war and there was much bloodshed and grief. The enemy was victorious and the way of life of a people was stamped out. The Coeur d'Alene were confined to one small portion of what had been vast ancestral land, a portion set aside for them in northern Idaho called a reservation.

There were hard times after the conquest and the advent of the reservation system. The goal of the government was to assimilate all Indians in the quickest, most efficient way possible. To this end the government established boarding schools and contracted with church schools. In Coeur d'Alene country, the government contract logically went to the Catholic church since they were already there.

The church, embraced long ago by the tribe, now became a cruel and efficient tool of assimilation. Almost all tribal members of my father's generation (he was born in 1892) learned to speak English and to read and write. His was the first generation to begin to wear shoes instead of moccasins.

My father and one of his brothers and many, many Indian men from many different tribes all over the country served in the United States Army in World War I. In 1924, partly in recognition of their service, the United States government permitted the Indian to become an American citizen.

My mother, who was my father's second wife, was not a Coeur d'Alene. She was Canadian and not a "status Indian" (that is, an Indian recognized as such by the government) because her father, to whom her mother was legally married, was a white (in this case, Irish) man. (Mixed-bloods with a white mother and Indian father, however, were recognized. That was the way it was in Canada.) Her mother was a Kootenay and a small part Chippewa. My mother spoke only English and was light-skinned and lived in white society all of her life until she married my father in about 1930 and made the Coeur d'Alene Reservation her home.

My father brought my mother to California to give birth

to me, the youngest of their children, in 1946. All the others, my three sisters and my brother who died as a baby, were born at home on the reservation. Mom had had a doctor attending only twice. Once only my father was there to assist. I think she was alone once. They didn't live in a town or even in a village, but way out in the countryside. They had no close neighbors. The house had no electricity because no power lines went out that far at the time and of course it had no indoor plumbing, no running water.

My mother was in her forties when she found out she was expecting me, and I was due in January. There were no hospitals or clinics near the reservation, and the temperature often dropped to forty degrees below zero in the winter and snow blocked the roads for weeks at a time. The boy my mother gave birth to the year before had only lived a few hours. They packed up a few suitcases and off the five of them went. My father was a carpenter and could work anywhere.

They drove and drove until they reached the place where it's never supposed to rain, let alone snow, the home of orange groves, palm trees and white beaches.

So I was born in Southern California but I don't remember it. At least not consciously. My mother used to tell me how the roar of the ocean disturbed her at night when we lived in Oceanside, made her feel uneasy somehow. But I have always loved the sound of the ocean. None of them liked the almost constant sunshine and the perpetual summer. They missed ice and snow and the sound of coyotes howling in the night. They missed home.

In June, when I was six months old, when northern Idaho's harsh winter had ended, my family packed up the car again and left sunny Southern California and went home to where their hearts were.

I first saw the light of day in California, but the first place I remember is our home in Idaho. There is no place on earth more beautiful than Coeur d'Alene country.

I always knew that Campbell is not a real whiteman name as it appears to be, not (like many "white" names Indian families have) just a name passed out by some government clerk who needed to write down a name and record an enrollment number after the treaties were signed and all the Indians had to be counted. Campbell is derived from my grandfather's father's Indian name.

And we Campbells are the last family left of the once powerful Turtle clan that was one of the Water People.

When I was ten years old, in 1956, my parents and I left our home reservation for the last time. None of us would ever live there again though my parents maintained strong ties. My father was active in tribal politics all of his life and never failed to vote in an election though he had to make a trip to Coeur d'Alene to do so since the tribe never permitted absentee ballots. Two of my sisters and their families returned after many years to live once more as part of the tribal community.

Thirty-six years after I left the reservation, in December of 1992, the Coeur d'Alene Tribal School (grades one through eight) invited me to visit. The school has been in existence for about twenty years.

I just visited the younger ones, saw their writing, heard them read, admired their artwork and the Christmas trees they had selected and cut and brought back to their classrooms to decorate.

I spoke to the oldest group, aged eleven through thirteen, which, as it turned out, included two great-nephews of mine. One I'd never met before. The other I'd not seen since he was about six years old.

The (white) teacher (all but one of the teachers were white) asked me if I were able to maintain my "ethnic identity" where I lived in New York. Or, he asked, was that important to me anymore. I answered that I am as Coeur d'Alene in New York as I am in Idaho, that it is something that is an integral part of me. I told the class to learn all they could about our history and culture because being a tribal person is something special, something non-Indian Americans don't have, and it can be a source of strength. It can provide a sense of continuity, of being connected to the land and to each other. Just think about it, I told them, how long our tribe has existed right here in this very place. Thousands of years. Many, many generations. We have survived as a tribal people for a long, long while. And, we're becoming stronger. When I was your age, I told them, there was no tribal school. There was no Tribal Enterprises or Tribal Farms. There were no privately owned Indian businesses back in those days as there are now. Today our tribe is waging a battle for the return of the illegally taken lakes. I didn't say anything about the poverty, the lack of employment opportunities, the high crime rate, the many social problems that plague modern reservations. Things are better now than when I was their age. I told them I spoke to a group of non-Indian high school students the week before and one of them told me she thought it "unfair" that Indians had to live on reservations. It had taken me a few minutes to figure out that the student thought Indians were forced to live on reservations the same way that people in South Africa had been. The native people of South Africa were allowed out during the day to go into the white cities and towns to work at low-level jobs but had to go back to their guarded, wretched reservations at night and that is the way some non-Indian people in America believe we have to live too. And that is sort of the way it was in the beginning. Indians had to give up buffalo hunting and root gathering and all the rest and stay put. But the government's intention all along was to get us to assimilate into the mainstream of America and to a large extent we have. We all speak English today and we go to school and we work and pay taxes. We drive cars and watch television and see all the big movies (if we want to). The government would like nothing better, at this point, than to abolish the reservations and get all our tribes to disband, to get rid of us. Only the reservation is our landbase, our home, and we don't want to let go of it.

I told them how I'd often heard non-Indians say they didn't know why Indians make such a big deal out of cultural retention. Why not be like other Americans? Like the Irish or Italian communities, for instance, who have big Saint Patrick's Day or Columbus Day celebrations once a year and then, for the most part, forget about their ethnic identities. The most important difference is this: if Irish or Italian culture dies in America it really isn't that big a deal. They still exist in Italy and Ireland. Not so with us. There is no other place. North America *is* our old country. And you kids, you are the future of our people.

Their teacher said something about my being a good role model. I don't know whether or not they bought it. I hope they didn't. I'm not a role model. At least not in the conventional sense.

If this were not a school visit, if I were with these children in a different context, I might say a few things more. I would say that yes, tribal identity and commitment to the community and family ties are important. But some of you kids, like me and like many other people from all kinds of racial and ethnic backgrounds, don't come from families that can and will encourage and support you. Some families will, if they can, tear you down, reject you, tell you you are a defective person. You could end up brokenhearted and broken-spirited.

If you come from such a family and you have no one else to turn to, then you must, for the sake of your own sanity and self-respect, break free, venture out on your own and go far away. Then you will have to rely on yourself and what you've managed to internalize regarding strength, stamina, identity and belonging.

Sometimes it will take a lot of courage to want to live and do well in spite of it all. But being courageous is part of our heritage. The most admired quality among the old Coeur d'Alene was courage. Courage has been bred into you. It's in your blood.

"This is your home," the tribal school's one Indian teacher told me before I left that afternoon. (It was her home, too.) "You be sure and come home again." I said of course. I would always come back.

At the time of my visit to the Coeur d'Alene Tribal School, I was Visiting Distinguished Professor of Creative Writing and Literature at Eastern Washington University, which is twenty-five miles west of Spokane and about a hundred miles from the reservation. I had just completed this book, my first work of nonfiction. It is a collection of autobiographical essays, not a single long work. In some of the pieces I try to articulate my experiences growing up in a dysfunctional family, to say this is how it was, this is what happened to me, this is how it made me feel.

The book is in part an effort to understand the pathology of the dysfunction, what made my family the way it was. I examine my own life in part, but reach beyond what I personally know or could know . . . back along my bloodlines to imagine the people I came from in the context of their own lives and times.

The most difficult piece to write was "Daughter of Winter," which is about my relationship with my mother, whom I loved, whose approval I always wanted but never had, who endured a great deal of pain and suffering in her own life. It was my mother who helped free me to write such a piece, though I know she didn't realize that was what she was doing.

When I was twenty-three and writing my first novel, *The Owl's Song*, I told my mother I was stuck. I was afraid of writing something that would offend people. The protagonist's family was poor and the father and the sister drank a lot. Things like that. I was torn between writing a novel that was true to my own vision and one that presented a positive image of Indian people.

My mother, who only went to grade three and almost never read novels, told me, "Maybe I'm just ignorant, but I thought it was a writer's business to write the truth as she sees it. Isn't it? What is the point of writing, why would anyone even want to do it if she's going to just write some nonsense to please someone else?"

One of the last times I saw my mother was in September of 1987, on her eighty-third birthday. I stopped by her house in central Washington en route to the memorial feast of her old best friend and sister-in-law, the woman who had introduced my parents to one another. Mom commented on how all she and my father's old friends were gone now and she named them. And now her best friend. She herself, she said, would have to be leaving pretty soon too. (She would die just six months later of ailments related to old age.)

My mother did something as we spoke I'd never seen her do before: she lapsed as old people frequently will. She forgot where she was, that she was in her own house in Wapato, Washington. She thought she was back in Idaho on the Coeur d'Alene Reservation . . . and *she forgot who I was.* She spoke to me as though I were a disinterested listener, the way she might speak to a nurse, a nun, a nursing home attendant, a roommate in a hospital.

"When I first came out here, I'm telling you it was a terrible time. A bad time in my life. She [her sister-in-law who had just died] was the only friend I had in the world."

My mother had married a white man when she was just sixteen and was unhappy in this marriage. "He had," she said, "no music in his soul. No joy. Nothing good. Nothing." She didn't expect love. She didn't believe in romantic love, not even as a young girl. She was glad to get married, though, and get away from home. She'd had to quit school after grade three to stay home and help take care of the younger ones and help with the housework. She thought marriage would be better than her life at home. Only it was a bleak, desolate existence with that man who hated music, who it turned out, hated Indians, too, though he knew when he married Mom that her mother was an Indian. He called my white-looking mother "squaw" and other derogatory names. She had two children by this man, a son and a daughter. She stayed married to him for ten long years.

Then she decided to get away for a little while and she went out to Idaho to visit her friend who had recently married a Coeur d'Alene tribal member. It happened that her friend's new brother-in-law came by the house to visit while my mother was there.

Mom's voice took on a lighter quality when she got to this part. "This was Nick," she said. "We saw each other and we both knew right away . . ." She stopped then, lost in time, remembering that day long ago when she and Dad first met.

I could hardly believe what I had heard. After all the awful things she used to tell me about my father, things no child should hear, things I didn't want to hear but had to because I was powerless to make her stop. I was just a child and at her mercy, her unwilling little confidante (she had no other confidante).

Dad had been horrible and evil, according to her, a low-down, no-good drunkard who had beaten her time and time again. . . . See this scar . . . she would say . . . see this one? She would show me her face. I would say yes but I never really saw. I never really looked. I focused my eyes at a point on her forehead instead and said, yes, I see. He was an evil brute, she said.

My father, the man I knew, did not resemble the violent monster of her horror stories in any way except for the fact that he did drink (but controlled it fairly well through most of my growing up years. He would go on a binge about every six months. Several times he went a whole year without a drink) and when he drank, yes, he was irresponsible. But my father, unlike my mother, was a gentle person. He was soft-spoken and generous. He very rarely raised his voice, let alone his hand, in anger, despite that ugly, spiteful mouth of hers that would not stop. And when they got old and arthritis crippled her, he was the one who took care of her needs and did everything he could to make her comfortable . . . until he died.

The beatings that she would not forget or forgive had all occurred long before my birth. I think I wouldn't have believed her (I didn't *want* to believe)—I might have thought she lied to justify her own behavior or for some other reason known only to herself. But my oldest sister, who is fourteen years my senior, remembered our father battering our mother when Mom had three small girls, no money, no one to help her, no chance of running away. She told me, when I was in my early twenties, how she had feared and hated our father for what he did . . . how he blackened Mom's eyes and bloodied her nose in his drunken rages.

My oldest sister, when she was just seven years old, decided she would kill our father in order to rescue Mom and rid them all of the misery he inflicted on their lives. She thought and thought and came up with a plan: when he came home late at night, she would run to the kitchen and get the iron skillet, then hide behind the kitchen door (which opened inward). This was where the fights always took place, for some reason—in the kitchen.

As she talked I imagined my sister at the age of seven, lying awake into the night listening, waiting for his return, then, when she heard the car pull up, sneaking downstairs, slipping unseen with her skillet behind the door in her flannel nightgown and her feet bare. I imagined her watching our parents through the crack in the door as our father hit our mother in the face with his big fists, holding her by the hair. And she, a strong woman, fought him, tried to get away. My sister saw it all up close as they moved around the room. She waited for him to be in precisely the right position—right in front of her hiding place—his back turned to her as he beat our mother. Then she would step out, the heavy skillet held above her head with both hands, and bring it down with all her might—crack!—on his skull and all that stuff would be over forever. Only Dad was never in exactly the right position. And after a few times of hiding and waiting for her chance that never came, my sister lost her nerve and gave it up.

Not long after, he reformed. Just like that. The beatings, all of the violence stopped about seven years before my birth. But Mom never forgave him. She was bitter all of their life together . . . and years and years after his death, still spoke of the things he'd done.

And yet, here she was, in her eighty-third year, recalling with tenderness the day they met: "We saw each other and we both knew right away."

"What, Mom?" I said when she didn't go on. "What did you both know right away? That you loved each other? Did you fall in love at first sight?"

Her eyes met mine and in an instant she snapped back, reoriented to time and place. She knew who I was now and was annoyed at me for asking such a question and at herself for having told me these things.

"No," she said, "I didn't fall in love!" As though that were the most ridiculous notion she'd ever heard. But I wouldn't drop it.

"Then what? What did you know right away?" She looked as though she were either going to not answer me or tell me it was none of my damned business.

But then she said, very softly, "We both knew that whatever was going to happen . . . was going to happen." And that was the end of it. She closed her eyes and spoke no more. Maybe she went to sleep.

Mom left her first husband for my father. In cases like that, in the 1930s, a mother always lost her children. Especially if the husband she left were white and the woman half-Indian and the man she ran off with a full-blood and the place she ran to was an Indian reservation. Especially if this all took place in a conservative place like Spokane, where racist attitudes towards Indians ran high. (Spokane is surrounded by Indian country, and there were no other racial or ethnic minorities in the area at the time.)

I think my parents started out loving each other. I think they had miserable times as the years passed (most, but not all, related to his drinking). And, I think maybe their love survived in spite of all of it, though in a crippled form. Nothing ever happened to set things straight. (Maybe nothing could.) Their family, the one I was born into, was a troubled one.

I used to have an old black-and-white photograph of my family: my parents, my three sisters, and myself, the only one ever taken of us together before any of us married or had children, when we were all still living with our parents.

This photograph was taken in 1946 in Tijuana, Mexico, just before we left California and went back to Idaho. We went there to buy nylon stockings for my mother, as nylons were very scarce in the U.S. during and just after the war.

When we got there, though, my father announced his intention to win free drinks at "The Longest Bar in the World." If anyone could sit on every barstool and have one drink, and still be able to stand when the last one was finished, all of his drinks would be on the house. It was impossible for anyone to have that many drinks and still be alive, let alone standing. Many had tried. No one had ever made it to the last barstool. My father said he would be the first and he went into The Longest Bar in the World.

But he came out a few minutes later, having had just one *cerveza*. He didn't feel like it, he said. Maybe another day. That day there were other things to do. We found a vendor and my mother bought four pairs of nylons. We did touristy things. A good time was had by all.

We had our picture taken on a set that looked like a covered wagon with a little burro hitched to it. My mother, father and two older sisters, then thirteen and fourteen, sit together side by side on the board seat of the wagon. My father holds me, a bright-eyed little baby, on his knee. My youngest sister, a beaming, apple-cheeked ten-year-old, sits on the burro.

My two older sisters, who have just recently passed from childhood into young womanhood, seem to be posing just a bit, trying to affect a little glamour. Both are wearing lipstick so dark it appears black in the photo. My middle sister is on the far left. She is the one I loved so much as a young child, the one who drew paper dolls for me, which we would color and cut out together, the one who would read Little Lulu comic books to me over and over again until I memorized all the dialogue verbatim and could fake people into thinking I could read. She bought me a beautiful Raggedy Ann doll with her first paycheck from her first job, which was, I think, at a Five and Dime, and got in trouble with Mom over it, for "throwing money around." (I was five years old when my middle sister married and left home. I wept and would not kiss her or even tell her good-bye. It hurt that she would leave me. We would never be close again, I thought. And I was right.) She is very thin in this photo. She had already been through a long, severe bout of TB and would be sick again in another few years and have to return to the sanitarium. But she doesn't look sick here. She looks fine.

My oldest sister is seated between my father and my middle sister. She is the family beauty (she would actually be, for a brief time, a small-time beauty queen and ride on floats and wear tiaras and wave to people on the sidelines). She never looked beautiful in photographs, though, and this one is no exception. But, like my other sisters, she looks young and innocent, fresh and pretty.

My youngest sister, according to my middle sister, had had a sweet, easygoing personality. She never did in my memory. But looking at the smiling ten-year-old on the burro in Mexico, it isn't hard to believe.

My mother is still pretty here. Her hair, mostly hidden by a sombrero with "Tijuana" written on the front, isn't grey yet. Her eyes are large (and you can tell they aren't dark because all of us, in the photo, have black, black eyes) and her lashes are thick and dark. She has a pretty mouth, a happy smile. She is Irish-pretty, not at all what anyone would call "exotic." She does not look nonwhite. She isn't yet overweight, as she would be all of the years I was growing up, but she has lost the slimness of her youth. She is "full-bodied" and she does look her age.

My father, surrounded by his family, looks silly in a som-

brero that says "Just Married" on it. He is handsome in a
rugged sort of way. He looks strong and vigorous. He is in
his mid fifties but looks ten years younger. His shirt sleeves
are rolled up to his elbows and his forearms are muscular
and smooth. I look very small sitting there on his knee, his
big hand holding me, and I look like I feel very secure. My
eyes are almond-shaped. My hair is very thick for a small
baby's, a wild mop.

We are smiling in Tijuana, having a good time. A happy,
handsome family. No one here is sick or old. The sun is
shining on us that spring day in Mexico in 1946. What I
wouldn't give to be able to set everything right for us from
that moment on.

What if Dad had walked out of the Longest Bar in the
World that day a changed man, what if he had experienced
an epiphany in there as he downed his Mexican beer . . .
realized exactly what he was doing and had been doing and
what he had to do in order to stop and told our mother,
when they were alone that night, that he would never take
another drink. And what if he hadn't.

And what if Mom, in time, had truly forgiven him and
trusted him and finally allowed herself to love him again just
like she had when the two of them first laid eyes on one
another and knew right away?

Or, what if Dad hadn't stopped drinking but Mom had
been able to support herself in some other way than she did
when she left him (as a scrubwoman, a fruit-picker, a hotel
maid). Say, as a teacher, a nurse, a photographer? She could
have had more than brief respites. She could have made a
life for herself. What if she hadn't suffered from rheumatoid
arthritis? What if her own family had been happier and

stronger and more supportive? What if. What if things had been different.

They weren't. *What if* does not exist. There is nothing but what was and is and we're all stuck with that and have to struggle to do our best with the hand we've been dealt. It has to do. It's all we have.

In 1987 I had a dream about a turtle. (We are the last family left of the Turtle clan.) A dream, in other words, about the family.

I am walking along the shore of a lake or a bay towards a house in the distance. I step on a small turtle I did not see lying among the rocks and think I've killed it. I am filled with grief. I leave it there and hurry away towards the house. I come back to that place on the shore later and see that the turtle is not only alive but is no longer the size of a small rock. It has grown to a hundred times its previous size. It's like a giant sea turtle and is very strong. I am filled with joy now. I watch as the great turtle walks into the water and swims away.

The dream was saying that our family only appeared to be dead, stepped on, broken into a million little pieces. The family—or the power of the family—lives on in some form and is strong. The dream didn't make sense. It was only an expression of my longing. My unconscious would not, after all these years, accept what I knew to be true. *The family isn't dead,* it said. *Give it up,* I said. *Let it go.*

In late 1992, just days before *Bloodlines* was to go into print, a niece I hadn't seen for fifteen years called me at Eastern Washington University and left a message on my answering machine. *This is your niece* (she said her name). *I would love to see you. Please give me a call if you would like to get together.* Her voice was still familiar to me after all these years. I played the message several times, listening to her voice, remembering. She is only seven years younger than I am. That was a lot when I was a child. She was my little baby doll then. I'd seen her only a few times after I left home at the age of fifteen. It wasn't my intention to see any family members while I was at Eastern. I wasn't going to contact any of them. I'd wanted to leave that door closed. They can't hurt me, I thought, as long as I stay away. *This is your niece. I would love to see you.* I picked up the phone and called her. She would take the day off work on Friday, she said, and come out to see me.

She did and didn't look the same as I remembered. I was amazed (though I shouldn't have been) to see that she was approaching middle age. And her resemblance to me was jarring. Same eyes. Similar facial bone structure. I looked at her and saw the family I came from. She had brought along her little ten-year-old daughter (who resembled her) whom I'd never seen before. The three of us spent the day together: shopping at a mall, having lunch. I treated my great-niece to a professional haircut and style (French braid), the first one she'd ever had. My niece and I spoke as we waited.

My niece, at thirty-nine, was a person who had developed herself, learned through a long process to trust her own perceptions. We talked about the family and how dysfunction begets dysfunction.

She had written a master's thesis about dysfunctional families and how the dysfunction gets passed down from one generation to the next. Not intentionally. But it does get passed down. It almost has a life of its own. She told me how she and some of her siblings and cousins discussed their own healing, their desire to break the cycle. She and some of the others made efforts to love one another and reach out to family members. "The family is so important," she said. "Sometimes I reach out and I'm rebuffed. Well, I just figure they're not ready. Everyone has to heal in their own time and in their own way. And I'm just going to keep on reaching out."

Once I longed to belong to the family I came from. Not anymore. I'm one of its broken-off pieces now. But this niece and others were trying to make what's left of it strong again. I would like to believe the family has the power to regenerate itself. I told my niece about the dream I'd had that was about the family, the dream of the turtle.

Autobiography in Fiction

My mother and older sisters used to like to tell a story about how I thought I was writing a book the winter I turned four years old. I would write like this: *eeeee eeee eeee eeeeee ee eeeeeee eeee eeeee eeeee eeeeeeee eee eeeee eeeee* line after line, page after page until I had filled three Big Chief tablets.

Sometimes they would ask me to read from my work, and I would read something like this, "The little girl was sitting quietly at the kitchen table writing. Just then her big sister came into the room and asked her to read something of what she had written to her."

I was compulsive about it, they said. I had to write in my tablets every day.

I can still, in a fragmented way, remember that awful winter. My mother had taken me and my two teenaged sisters (the oldest one was married) and left my father, who was away from home at the time on "a bender." She had no resources, though, and no place to run to. We went to Medical Lake, Washington, and lived with my mother's sister and her family. It was very cold, and we were isolated in the country. In my memories of that winter it is always blizzarding.

I can remember writing in those tablets, too, though I can't remember what I wrote. I remember opening myself up and focusing all my energy, channeling it into the "writing." I didn't understand then what writing was, that letters represented different sounds and, put together, they made words that were symbols that stood for thoughts and feelings and objects in the physical world.

In my four-year-old's mind I believed reading and writing worked more or less like this:

The writer, when she makes the marks upon the paper, must concentrate very, very hard, must put everything she has into this making of marks, must think the thoughts and feel the feelings deeply and intensely because it would be through this intensity that the thoughts of the writer would be transferred from the writer's mind onto the paper. Then, if the writer had managed to leave her emotions and thoughts in the marks on the paper, a reader could come along and pick up the paper and look at these marks and the reader could feel and think as the writer had when the writer wrote on the pages. The thoughts and feelings would remain as long as the marks remained on the paper, or as long as the paper would last.

I think that that was not very different from the way I would write later on, after I had learned to read and write in the conventional sense, as a teenager expressing myself in poetry no one would ever read and much later as an adult writer of novels. If it is to be real and true, if you are to write the deep-down truth and have it understood the way you intend, then you must concentrate all your energy, must throw off pretensions and bare your soul, write with the utmost sincerity and intensity whatever it is you want to say, right down to your very core.

I don't remember what it was I wrote about that winter at Medical Lake when I filled three Big Chief tablets with writing. I like to think it was something more than reportage, though, that I was in some way interpreting life, giving some order to the chaos my life had become, and in this writing was keeping my own counsel.

The More or Less Autobiographical Story
I Will Write From My Sickbed
at St. Luke's Hospital

A friend has brought me a notebook and a pen, and I am to write a story. If it turns out I can't write a story after all, or if I do but it isn't any good, that will be okay because I am lying in my sickbed. I am in fact really doing this for therapeutic, not artistic reasons.

My story will be, of course, autobiographical, more or less—in a manner of speaking—and after it gets famous, people will ask me if it is. And I'll think, How tiresome, and try to think of something literary to say, knowing it really won't matter what I say.

Something literary like "Not autobiographical in a literal sense, but I suppose it is in the same way that everything one writes is in some way based on his or her own personal vision of life. But fiction is concerned with a higher truth."

It won't matter what I say because most people want to believe that it is, indeed, the author's own life that is displayed in such naked, intimate, detail for public viewing. I, as a writer, will have been concerned with the verisimilitude of the story, will have taken pains to make my characters and their situations seem real (and to accomplish this end, I do things like have one protagonist go to law school, have another live on the Northwest Coast—not because I want to write about myself but because I know through personal experience what it is like to be in law school. I know what it feels like to live in a place where I am awakened by the sound of the surf, and it rains most all of the time, and dramatic, snow-capped mountains are a daily presence. Interviewers often remark on how my characters' lives "parallel" my own despite the "claim" that what I write is not autobiography. Yet, really, it is by sharing my own experiences with my fictional characters that I am able to breathe life and authenticity into them).

One plot-developing exercise I assign my creative-writing students is to bring in short news stories from a daily paper and then, from the bare bones of such a story, develop a plot, then flesh it out into a story.

Someone will always remind me, "But you said we write from our own experience," as though such a statement were contradictory to the assignment.

I say, "None of us knows how anyone else perceives the world, what another person feels or thinks. We only know what we ourselves feel and think and what others tell us of their experience. In fiction we create the illusion that we can know what someone else knows and feels. We attempt to share our experience with others through our work.

"Suppose you have a character in your story walk down the road and you describe his feelings as he does this. The feel of a light rain on his face, the gravel under his shoes, the sound of a car engine in the distance. See, you really only know those things from your own experience . . . how the gravel feels beneath your shoes as you walk over it. You give your experience to your characters. That does not mean, however, that they are you."

My story, I think, will be about a woman who, like me, was born in 1946. As the story opens, in late 1986, she has been through almost a year of mourning for her lost youth. She wants to stop mourning, to settle into middle age.

Then you won't have to worry about grey hair or crow's-feet, not being noticed (*really* noticed) anymore by men. Then you won't care so much because you will have arrived into a new era in your life. You'll be "accepting," you'll settle in, you won't bark or whine or wish it weren't true. You'll just *be* middle-aged.

So let's give this forty-year-old woman a name. Julia is fine. And a life. A life, sort of, more or less, like my own.

She is, like me, a writer, and this is the first year she has ever tried to live as a full-time writer, to not have any other kind of employment. She has only recently begun to realize the seriousness of her work . . . that is, that it is through her work that she keeps herself together. Through her work she struggles to define herself and her reality. Like me, she lives alone and is divorced. But I have two children while she has none.

She lives in a small, old town on the Washington coast. Maybe Bellingham. Maybe not. Maybe a meshing of Bellingham and Neah Bay with a dash of Port Townsend thrown in.

Her town will be, like Bellingham, a commercial fisherman's town. (Port Townsend is much too trendy.) Georgia-Pacific paper mill is a nice touch, I think, very smelly, and we know by its presence that this is a working-class town. Yet Bellingham also contains a large enclave of yuppies, and that is not the way I want her town to be.

I want her to feel as I feel at Neah Bay,* at earth's end.

*Neah Bay, home of the Makah Indians, is a village at the old site of Ozette, at the tip of the Olympic Peninsula, as far north and west as you can get and still be in the continental United States.

(You see the metaphor, don't you? She is at her own earth's
end—no husband or prospect of one. No lover. No children,
approaching the end of her childbearing years. And though
her work has enjoyed some critical attention, she, unlike
myself, has not published with major presses, has not received award nominations and wide critical acclaim. The
year she has decided to spend writing is a "This is it—it's
now or never" sort of thing.)

Land's End may be the name of her town. Or Earth's
End. I also like the isolation of Neah Bay, how mud slides
make the road impassable during the winter, and I like the
way sea lions loll casually about on the rocks there, and I
would like to have them in my story.

The house she lives in is a hundred years old, is musty-
smelling and poorly insulated. It belongs to Julia's friend,
whom she first knew when they were thirteen years old and
at boarding school. Let's call her friend Mona.

Mona's aunt died in the house several months before
Mona told Julia she could come live there.

It once belonged to Mona's grandparents, and Mona
visited there often as a child.

Mona comes to the house to pack away her aunt's belongings in the first days that Julia is there. Mona needs Julia's
company as she sorts through the old woman's things. She
needs to tell an interested, sympathetic person about her
aunt's life and some of her own memories connected with
the house.

Mona tells her, by the way, there are a good many snakes
around here—lurking all over in the overgrown grass . . .
that ugly, black kind you see around these parts, sometimes
with yellow stripes running down their backs.

Once, Mona tells her, when she was a little girl, she came upon a startling sight in the backyard: a mother snake with her brood of squirming, writhing, intertwining baby snakes.

Julia resolves never to go in the backyard. She won't even go out there to hang laundry on the line. She wonders if a man would allow himself to be intimidated by snakes, or if he would be afraid but not admit that he was out of a need to preserve his macho self-image.

Julia may only live in the house until the estate is probated. Maybe it will be six or seven months. No longer than nine months.

Julia sets up her desk by the window in the living room and arranges her writing materials. She writes letters to people and tells them of her "studio," how the window in front of the desk overlooks the bay and she watches the fishing boats going out and coming in . . . and the occasional tall ship. She walks on the beach every day as a proper writer would. Now I am a real writer, she tells herself, no longer an overworked social worker trying to sneak in an hour's writing time here and there.

Julia also has a drinking problem. I don't think I will go into it much, beyond just letting the reader know that it is connected to Julia's melancholy and she is afraid of it taking her over as it took over her brother after his return from Vietnam.

When Julia was in Seattle, still working at her social worker's job, she wrote Mona a letter about her need for peace, how she wanted to write but had neither time nor energy after her grueling day's work at Child Protective Services.

About the drinking she wrote, "It isn't a matter, anymore,

of it being an embarrassment, of feeling like I am a weak person for using it to help me make it through the night. I wish that that were all it was.

"It's much more now. It's as though I leave myself each time I drink and something evil takes hold. I'm not talking about Dr. Jekyll and Mr. Hyde stuff. I don't mean that I do wicked, damaging things, that I steal or hurt or kill or anything. I mean it feels like *I* am what the alcohol wants. Me. And each time I leave myself, the evil grows stronger. I have to not drink. I've got to. Somehow I must stop or, like Doc Holliday at the O.K. Corral, I will have to prepare to forfeit my soul."

Mona, who is her oldest friend, wrote her a letter the same day she received Julia's letter and said, "Come here. Live in the old house for a while. Write. Search for a better job. Catch your breath." Julia now has begun a novel, which is progressing well. She hasn't had a drink in six months.

A distancing process has occurred. I have become Julia. I can see her, and she is not me.

Though she is my age she is older-looking than I, and plainer than I am (or at least than I imagine myself to be). I am taller than average. Quite tall, in fact, but I don't want her to be. She is just average height. Rather dumpy-looking.

She has heavy hips and thighs, large feet. She has short arms and a rather frail upper body, narrow shoulders, and rib cage. Large breasts.

I imagine Julia examining her breasts in the mirror. How they have changed since her youth, she thinks. Is it noticeable when she is dressed how they have changed? Do people who see her walking along the street assume she has middle-aged breasts, no longer plump and bouncy beneath her bra, turtleneck, sweatshirt?

She wears a red cotton bandana over her dark hair, tied behind at the nape of her neck. Her hair has begun to turn grey. She will not dye it because long ago she promised herself she would never be so vain as to dye her hair.

I see her as rather ruddy-complexioned ("Irish skin," women with that kind of skin like to say). The kind of woman who can't walk on the beach for long when the sun is out and who must keep moving her position outdoors to follow the shade because her skin is too sensitive to sunlight.

Either I will make no mention of her race or she is just a white-looking Indian. I don't think race will be an issue . . . or maybe it will. Two marriages. One abortion. No children.

For years Julia owned a big black Saint Bernard–Labrador named Bjorn, whom she loved, who died, whom she misses.

She dreams about Bjorn. She wishes he were there to walk on the beach with her, to lie at her feet while she reads or writes, to reach down and touch.

Stories aren't written as a series of intellectual decisions. It is an intuitive sort of thing.

The intellect controls, selects, and rejects, yet the story doesn't come from the intellect. It is brewed in the unconscious—fiction comes from the deeper, darker places in the writer's soul, the same places that dreams come from, and, as in the making of dreams, the unconscious makes use of bits and pieces as it weaves its fiction tapestry: autobiography, yes, if there is anything there that can be used, and other people's works, both fiction and fact, all that you experience.

Fiction speaks in symbolic language, symbols both personal and universal. Fiction and dreams spring from a common well. Dreams, though, speak to the individual—draw attention to suppressed needs, answer troublesome questions, make clear to the dreamer that which was clouded.

In the practice of fiction, artists speak not only to the self but to others as well. Fiction illuminates, imposes order where there was none. Where autobiography, so-called, is used as a basis for fiction, a rearrangement, a transformation must occur.

I first became aware of how compelling this "rearrangement" is in my writing when someone from the University of Nebraska Press wrote me and asked me to submit a short autobiography for inclusion in an anthology of writers' autobiographies.

I began writing what I intended to be an honest, sincere, real story about my life.

Before I knew it, I was writing about Carmen Miranda and how, when I was a little girl, I'd wanted to grow up to be just like her, and I had Carmen Miranda paper dolls and coloring books and used to fantasize about Carmen Miranda being my real mother . . . that one day she would come to reclaim me, and I'd drawn a picture of Carmen and myself embracing and wrote a caption, "Mother and Daughter Reunited," and tacked it to the wall above my little bed.

I was aware of lying, yet I couldn't stop myself . . . no, I didn't care to stop myself. All this stuff about Carmen

Miranda was a lie. I'd liked her quite a lot, but that was all. (And if it had been the way I wrote about it I doubt that I would have wanted to tell anyone about it, let alone state it in writing for publication.)

And the real-life drawing was this: When my daughter was about ten, she was to leave me to go spend the summer with her father. This would be our first long separation, and I was feeling sad and knew how deeply I would miss her.

She drew a picture of the two of us embracing, wrote the caption "Mother and Daughter Reunited" and taped it to the wall. This was for me to look at when I got lonesome so that I could remind myself that she would be coming back.

So there were elements of truth in the passage about Carmen Miranda, but the passage was not the truth. And I didn't know why I was writing those things, but I went on with it anyway.

When I finished and read it over, I saw immediately that this was really the material I needed to go into the novel I was then writing, *The Jailing of Cecelia Capture.*

If it were autobiography the whole passage would be a pack of lies. But it was not autobiography at all, but fiction, you see. I used it in my novel and decided against writing an autobiography for the University of Nebraska anthology.

I don't get an idea for a story and then set about writing the story. I've got to let the story have its own way. I see myself, then, as the servant of my fiction rather than as using my fiction as a vehicle to convey my predetermined "message."

For instance, when I was in intensive care, watching my

heart beat thump its way across the screen, I thought, as I think many people do in similar circumstances, about my own mortality, about how fleeting life is. I thought of all the things I haven't done yet, how much I still wanted to do and see. I thought of patching up differences. If I ever get out of here, I thought, I will be different. I thought of how I would like to write a story in which I would share my new insights with others.

I would like to write a story like this: A forty-year-old woman, when she is seriously ill, suddenly understands how she hadn't been living life to the fullest. She resolves that when she gets out of the hospital, she is going to do all these good works: visit old people's homes, donate money to orphanages, call old friends she has been neglecting for a long time. Maybe she will attempt to reconcile with a sister or other relative from whom she has been estranged for years. But she can't do any of these things because she dies in the hospital. Then the story would be about life before it's too late. Or maybe she gets well and gets out of the hospital and forgets how she felt in her time of crisis and goes back to being ordinary and selfish.

I knew, though, even as I imagined such a story, that it would never see the light of day because it had no life of its own.

Although acquiring a deep appreciation of life and wanting to live life for all it was worth was a deeply meaningful experience on a personal level, it was not the stuff stories are made of. It would be a mere contrivance. I would have to fashion a story to convince my reader of my point of view.

I would have to attempt to manipulate the emotions of my reader, and this is not the way honest fiction is written.

Getting back to my Julia in her creaky old house at Earth's End: I will have to work with her, let her story emerge. Thus the vague, intangible, gnawing feelings, the haunting images, are allowed to see the light of day, are given form, are brought into tangible existence.

This is how writers articulate their own vision and create a means through which that vision can be shared with other people.

Not so simple, then, as "autobiography," is it? Real life comes into play only insofar as it can serve the purpose of art.

An old woman has been admitted to the room across the hall. She is very old, very thin and fragile-looking. I keep getting up and closing the door so I won't have to see her as she lies in bed in her darkened room in the light from the TV screen, because the sight is so disturbing to me. The nurses keep reopening the door. The old woman wears a lime-green crocheted cap.

The image of the frail old woman in a green cap staring at TV haunts me, even in my sleep. She is always alone. No one ever visits. Maybe she will find her way into my fiction one day. Maybe not. Making fiction is a mysterious process.

My
Half Brother's
Mother

Was there a light in the closet? Did he have a toy to play with while he waited? Or did he huddle in the darkness listening to the sounds his mother made turning a trick (or whatever it was called back then), doing what she could to pay the hotel-room rent and buy food for the two of them?

The year would be 1920 or '21—not a good time for a woman to be on her own with a child to support, and she, my father's first wife, was an Indian too (and therefore not a citizen, second-class or otherwise, of the United States of America*).

She was on her own with her little boy in the city (Spokane or Seattle, I'm not sure which) because what else could she do after the scandal? Where could she go? Her lover was dead and her husband in prison for killing him. Maybe she could have stayed on the reservation with her family, but she had disgraced them so.

She took her little boy and struck out on her own. Did she imagine she could get some kind of work in the city? Scrubbing floors or in a laundry or as somebody's maid? And, if she found work, who would take care of her child while she was at her job? She was all alone. I don't know if she even spoke any English. (I do know, though, that my half brother

*The United States government didn't make Indians citizens until 1924.

did not know English as a child.) She probably wouldn't
have been forced to attend mission school, as my father had
been, since she was a girl. Or maybe she was; I don't know.
If she knew English, I imagine she knew it only poorly.

What happened was she had a lover with whom she
intended to run away. Dad had gone away on a job and was
not expected back for days, but he came home early, and
there they were: his wife and her lover getting ready to leave,
packing the lover's car (which I imagine was black, weren't
most cars black in the 1920s, with running boards along the
sides?) They packed it with cardboard boxes, suitcases,
maybe some blankets.

Dad had his hunting rifle with him. He probably carried
it in case he spotted some game, a deer or maybe an elk, as
he drove along the road. He took that rifle and shot and
killed the man who would run off with his wife. He had to
go to prison then, but for only a year (or was it eighteen
months?).

Many years later, when he was a grown man, my half
brother would tell my mother, Dad's second wife, about the
time his mother took him to live in a hotel in the city and
how she managed to support the two of them. "She thought
I was too young to know what was going on," he said when
he got to the part about being put in the closet, "but she was
wrong." He didn't have many memories of her. That was
one.

Then she got sick. She had TB. Whether she had it before
she went to the city or contracted it there, I'm not sure.
When it got so bad she couldn't go on, she went back to the
reservation to her parents.

I know TB. When I was a little girl, one of my older sisters had it. I know the awful coughing that never stops, the spitting up of blood, the wasting away. But when my sister had it, she went to a sanitarium and was treated. My sister eventually recovered. My half brother's mother did not. In her day TB was always fatal.

Her mother tended her in her last days. I hope they all forgave her in the end for the terrible thing she did. When she died, they buried her in her own family's plot.

My father died many, many years later in March 1969. I was a student in California at the time. We buried him on the day of the first moon landing. I recall how cold Idaho seemed compared to California, the ground all covered with snow.

Before the Catholic Mass a wake and traditional memorial service were held in the tribal community hall. My half brother, my father's grey-haired son, was there.

On the wall of the community hall, in a display of photographs of tribal members in days gone by, was a photograph of my half brother and his mother.

My half brother is about two years old in the photograph. His mother, who looks about sixteen and can be no more than eighteen, holds him on her lap, her arms wrapped around him holding him close. She is dressed Indian style, her black hair parted in the middle and in two long braids. The photograph must have been taken about two years before the incident.

Did he remember still, I wondered, the way they were in that photograph? Young girl mother and infant son? And how her arms felt around him holding him close?

We buried my father in his family plot, his grave near the
grave of his first wife.

My mother, who outlived my father by nearly twenty
years, always said she preferred to be buried elsewhere. She
was.

Daughter
of Winter

It was an old frame house on West Eighth Street in the little Yakima Indian reservation town of Wapato, Washington. It used to be yellow when Mom and I lived there, but was now white with green trim. It had had two stories but now had only one (lost the upper story in a fire years ago, my mother told me later), and the big tree in the backyard, our yard, was gone. All that was left of that tree now was a short, grey, cracked stump.

We lived in the rear apartment. It was a housekeeping room, actually, just one small, narrow room with a sink, hot plate, fridge . . . a sofa that folded down into a bed, a little table and two wooden chairs. There was a tiny separate room with a toilet and shower stall. It was one of many, many places my mother and I lived while I was growing up.

I was twelve years old when we lived there. I don't recall how long, but I do know some of that time was in winter because our water pipes froze once. And I didn't have a coat or scarf, boots or gloves, no winter clothing of any kind. When it got really cold, my mother would let me wear her coat to school. It was warm but much, much too large, and it was worn and old and of a style an old woman, not a young girl, would wear. But I wasn't ashamed to wear my mother's coat to school (even though this was my first year of junior high). One thing about Wapato was that it was (and is, for that matter) full of poor people. I was just one poor, shabby kid among many.

We had a radio in our little apartment. Buddy Holly's "Peggy Sue" and Sam Cooke's "You Send Me" always remind me of living in that little cubbyhole.

I remember being hungry there too. Often our only meal would be boiled barley with a little salt and a pat of margarine.

I had planned on going to that place on a sort of sentimental journey. I imagined myself sitting on the steps again. If anyone lived there (which I rather doubted—how could such a place pass present-day housing inspection?), I would explain to the tenant that I had lived there a long time ago when I was a child and just wanted to visit the place for a moment.

I parked my car and walked up the alleyway to the back gate (the way I had gone to school and come back every day). I put my hand on the latch. A flood of sadness overwhelmed me. I could not lift the latch, could not make myself enter that yard. I stared at the house. Not so different despite the new white paint and the missing upper story and the cracked, aged stump where a beautiful tree had once flourished.

This is where I lived the winter I was twelve. What was I like then? What was I like? Could I have, did I, ever imagine an adult self standing at this gate? One who had a very different, much better life? Did I ever imagine a future for myself back then, seriously imagine, not just fantasize? I don't think so.

I left the building on West Eighth Street and went back to my mother's house on West Second, just ten short blocks away. I told her I'd gone there and stopped awhile.

"Do you remember how poor we were?" she asked me. Yes, of course I did. She had lived through many, many hard times, she said. That was one. Just one. I never appreciated her, never appreciated what she had gone through for my sake.

"What did you think about, Mom?"

"What?" she said, incredulously, as if that was the stupidest question she'd ever heard.

"What did you think about when we lived on West Eighth?" I meant, how had she felt during that time, how had she interpreted this

experience to herself? What sort of person had she been? What motivated her? But she took my question as a reproach, and this irritated her. She accepted no blame. None. Not ever. Not for anything. She didn't have to explain herself to anyone, least of all to me.

"What do you think I thought about?" she said, a mean, hard edge to her voice that I knew well (weakened though it was with illness and old age). "Just what do you think I thought about? I thought about where my next dollar was coming from. I thought about how I might get a hold of some potatoes, maybe a few onions. That's what I thought about it!" She would never discuss anything with me having to do with my early life with her. Unless she wanted to tell me what a horrid child I'd been. That made understanding all she'd done difficult. Very difficult.

I

If I were to make a video of my early years, from the time I was four or five to the age of ten, I would show, among other things, a montage of my mother and myself on the run, running from place to place all over the big states of Idaho, Washington, and Oregon. We're runnin' from Dad and his drinkin', which Mom had to tolerate for many years when the others were small. She won't anymore. We're runnin' towards a new beginning, a fresh start that somehow never pans out. Mom is fiftyish when the video begins, mid-fifties at the end. She looks quite a lot older than she is. She has grey, home-permed hair, wears cheap, soon-faded cotton housedresses. She weighs about two hundred pounds all through these and the remainder of my growing-up years.

One peculiar thing about us is my mother looks white (though she is actually a mixed-blood Indian) while I, like my father and older sisters, look Indian. I'm used to people asking me if I'm adopted. The other peculiar thing about us, besides the apparent racial difference, is that my mother is a generation older than the mothers of other children my age. I am also used to people asking me if Mom is my grandmother.

Our home base, more or less, is the isolated Coeur d'Alene Indian Reservation in northern Idaho, where my father and all his people were born, where all of my sisters were born and grew up (almost finished growing up). Except that they did live in California one year when I was born.

Then, when I am two (I don't remember this), my middle sister, who is fourteen years old at the time and a TB patient, has a relapse and goes into a sanitarium, Cushman Indian Hospital in Tacoma, Washington, just a few miles south of Seattle. Then we live in Tacoma on and off for a number of years. Dad works at McChord Field there. My two older sisters marry Puyallup Indians and establish family bases of their own in rural areas near Tacoma (my third sister will establish her base on the Yakima Reservation in central Washington, but that will come later, after the end of this video).

So, in this video of my early years (say, to promote an autobiographical song I'd written and recorded about Mom and me runnin' away from Dad and his drinkin'. Maybe I'd recorded a whole album of songs about this.) we would live in many different places but would return to our original home (but not Mom's original home) in Idaho several times, and in order to be near my two older married sisters, we would live in many different areas in or near Tacoma.

We never run when my oldest sister is still with us, and only two or three times when my middle and youngest sister are with us. We stay with relatives, live in a one-room shack in a migrant-labor camp with a communal water pump and communal outhouses. Mom and my middle and youngest sisters pick berries. I'm with them all day out in the field. The sun is hot. The dirt is plowed, it's deep and soft and hard to walk in. Slugs infest the strawberries (which grow close to the ground). Raspberries, which grow on vines trained on wires and posts, are better. Mom wears a big straw hat and a long-sleeved man's shirt while she works (her white skin burns in the sun. Our brown skin doesn't.). I pick berries and put them in a wooden box. I think I'm helping a little. One of my sisters tells me I'm no help at all, that I'm just a burden to them. I think a burden must be a little bird. I think she's telling me I'm no more help than a little bird would be. We (or they) make enough money to buy groceries. Our rent is free. Mom reads the Bible every evening before going to sleep.

Another time Mom has a job in an apple dryer. I don't know what that is, but I know that she has to stand at a conveyor belt all night long. She sleeps all day. I hardly get a chance to see her. My sisters are supposed to keep me away from her while she sleeps, but I give them the slip sometimes and go to her in the darkened room. Sometimes my sisters come in and get me and take me away. But sometimes Mom allows me to lie with her for a while, to lie in her arms. I'm happy then. She smells so fragrantly of apples: her clothes, her skin, her hair.

Just the two of us on the run by the time I'm seven. She works in various hotels as a maid. The Jim Hill is the name of one. She brings home little bars of soap. She also works as a scrubwoman in a nursing home, several different nursing homes. Once or twice she gets a much easier and better-paying job attending a terminally ill patient in their home. I don't know when I become aware—it seems like I always knew—that Mom has arthritis. Her own mother, Gram Sullivan, was crippled by a stroke. Being crippled is one of Mom's greatest fears, becoming dependent on others.

. Mom always wears nylon stockings . . . I don't know why she does . . . they have runs . . . full of runs. She has varicose veins. Pain in her back and in her knees. She works so hard. Scrubbing other people's floors. Making hotel beds. Cleaning hotel-room toilets. Arthritis gets worse and worse as time passes. Keeping active, though, helps keep it at bay.

We're so poor, Mom and me, so damned, damned poor. Sometimes I'm hungry. She always said I never went hungry and was always proud of that. "Come what may," she used to say, "you never went hungry." That isn't true. (Maybe what she meant by "not going hungry" was that I never went an entire day without eating, and that is true.) I remember being hungry at school, feeling faint. My hands tremble and I sweat, though it isn't warm. My head feels light. Or it hurts. I get headaches a lot when I'm little. Nosebleeds too.

We follow a rambling course all over the Northwest. Usually we go from one grubby little town to another, but sometimes not. Sometimes we stay in a city. We are never on welfare through any of this. Not once. Mom doesn't like welfare. As long as she's able to work, she says, she will.

Sometimes I find ways of making a little money: I shovel snow from people's walks. I make greeting cards and sell them door-to-door. (Amazingly people buy my little cards on notebook paper, drawn with crayon.)

We go back to Dad a lot, who reforms, but only for a time.

We aren't poor when we're with Dad (but neither are we what you would call well off). I hate to leave Dad. We always sneak off. Usually he's gone drinking when we sneak, but once in a while he's just at work and she decides to leave because she knows he's going to start drinking soon. (She can always tell when he's about to go on a bender, she says.) He calls this her "disappearing act."

Usually, especially when I'm very young, we run off on Greyhound buses. I have one memory of running away one winter night on a Greyhound: We're in the mountains and it's snowing very hard. It's very late at night, and I'm the only one awake. I'm on my knees on the seat that spans the width of the bus in the very back, looking out the window. Snow swirls behind the bus, is kicked up by the big tires . . . the snow, directly behind, is tinted red by the tail lights. Mesmerizing. Like the white foam behind a big ferry boat.

Mom always wants to be around my sisters. We sleep in their cars and in their garages and storage shacks, or on sofas in the living rooms of their overcrowded (because they all have many, many children) little houses or apartments.

I am still a little girl, but my sisters are now adults. One of them takes a snapshot of me eating soup to show me how awful I look, how uncouth and sloppy. In this photo I am seated at a table, a bowl in front of me. (I am six years old.) My mouth is open and I am leaning forward, holding a spoon and drawing it towards my mouth. I don't look particularly uncouth; I just look like a little girl eating soup: an odd subject for a photograph. It survived for decades. Maybe one of my sisters still has it.

Included in my video is an episode in which I am kicked out of the house by my mother when I am seven years old.

. . .

Mom and I live alone in a dumpy old two-room apartment
in Omak, Washington. (She asked God to tell her where to
go that time, then closed her eyes, opened the Bible, put her
finger on the open page and opened her eyes. She interpreted whatever it said to mean, "Go to Omak," so here we
are.) We've been here before. Omak is where the Jim Hill
Hotel is.

Mom kicks me out for telling her she will burn in purgatory if she doesn't stop swearing.

She sends me to Christ the King Elementary Catholic
School in Omak, even though I am the only Indian there. I
hate Christ the King and the awful kids and awful nuns who
grab me and pull me around. My arms are full of thumb-
shaped bruises from being manhandled.

A drunkard couple lives in the apartment next to ours (we
have to share a toilet down the hall with them and with a few
other tenants). Mom stays up late. She sits in the kitchen and
smokes and reads. Maybe the Bible. Maybe something else.
The library is free. Mom reads a lot. She makes me go to bed
early.

She and I share a double bed, and my place is against the
wall . . . a thin wall . . . which separates us from the wretched
couple, who drink and fight and throw furniture around all
night long. Sometimes they throw things, things that break,
against the thin wall that separates us. The wall I sleep next
to. They swear and curse "somethin' awful," as Mom would
say. Somethin' awful. Dirty, vulgar, vile language. I hate the
couple. Most of all the swearing. The swearing makes a lump
form in my throat so big, it's hard to swallow. And my chest
feels tight, like there's a weight on it. I never get to sleep until
very late. Then I get up and go to that stupid Christ the
King, where I am manhandled by sadistic nuns.

Then I come home to a mother who swears. Her whole family swears. My father does not. He always hated their swearing too. She swears at *me*. Because I left a towel in the bathroom. Because I forgot to hang up my school clothes. Because I'm me. I decide to tell her off. She's going to burn in purgatory, I tell her, unless she stops the swearing. For once my mother is dumbfounded. She doesn't know what to say at first. She is very, very angry.

She tells me that I am the one who will burn, not her, because I drove her to swear.

But this time I've got God on my side, the God she believes in so wholeheartedly along with the devil. "No, Mom, not me. *You!* Nobody but *you!*" The commandment, I point out, says, "Thou shalt not take the Name of Thy Lord Thy God in Vain." There is no commandment that says a word about not driving someone else to swear.

She gives me the silent treatment all evening. I feel strangely triumphant. I couldn't make the drunkard couple stop, I couldn't control the nuns at school. But I can get my mother to stop swearing.

The next morning I wake up to the sound of her singing (this is her lifelong trick when she wants to wake someone but doesn't want to do it directly). She's in good spirits, it sounds like. She's singing "Ragtime Cowboy Joe." She's in the kitchen ironing clothes. When she sees I'm up, she begins folding the clothes . . . *my* clothes . . . and putting them into the open suitcase she has sitting on a chair beside the ironing board.

This is the suitcase I use when we run away. It's little and it's made of cardboard and it has some kind of brown tweedy design on paper glued to it.

"Since you're so dissatisfied with me as your mother, you

can leave," she tells me, closing the suitcase, snapping the metal fasteners in place and handing it to me. "Go on now. Get the hell out of here." She's smiling. I pick up the suitcase. It isn't very heavy, but I'm only seven years old.

The outside steps are narrow and steep. I manage, holding onto the railing and going down one step at a time.

Then I wander, carrying the suitcase. Don't know what to do. Don't know where to go. I walk along the dirt road that runs beside the Okanagan River. Everyone knows bums sleep under the bridge that crosses that river. I can too. But what about food? Maybe I can go around town finding new kids to play with every day. Maybe their mothers will invite me when it gets to be suppertime and I'm still there. Finally my head is aching, aching from trying to think of a plan, trying to think of ways I can survive. I sit down on the ground and cry. When I am finished, my head hurts more than ever. I know I have to go home and humiliate myself as I never have before. I have to go beg my mother to take me back.

She makes me admit that I broke the commandment that says "Honor Thy Father and Thy Mother" when I criticized her for swearing. (I confess that sin when I make my first Confession.)

My video will show a map of all the places I lived. I attended twenty-one schools in three states before I dropped out of school after eighth grade. No, I went a month or two in tenth. Then there were the places we lived before I began school and where we lived in summer when school wasn't in session, and places I simply did not attend school even though it was in session. How many places were there in all? Where did I live while I was growing up? When someone asks me that, I always experience a little anxiety. Such a common, simple question: Where did you grow up? Where are you from? Most of the time I just say L.A., since I was born near there and nobody wants to get into a conversation about L.A. Sometimes I say from Idaho because that is where my home was . . . the home of the tribe I belong to.

Some of the places I lived while I was growing up are only dim memories now, and they tend to run together and blur a little bit: the cabin in Lewiston, Idaho, where just Mom and I live. It's winter (but it isn't very cold because in all of Idaho, Lewiston is the town with the lowest elevation), and I am very young. I'm sure not five yet. Mom has to tell me not to play on the floor because it's too cold. She keeps picking me up and putting me on the bed. She goes to the store and leaves me alone, but I'm not scared or anything. She probably does this because she has no car and we live a long way from a store and she can't carry me and groceries too. I remember she keeps buying me the same Frosty the Snowman comic book (she forgets she already bought it). Then there is a long, dark, narrow apartment in Tacoma in an old building that is covered on one side with ivy and morning-glory vines. It's next door to a Buddhist temple. The Buddhists chant. Sometimes their chanting is eerie. My mother has a friend in that building who is black and whose name is Belle. In Yakima a long, cabinlike duplex with a bathroom in the middle we share with the family who lives on the other end. The summer is scorching hot. I run through the sprinklers in the shady park behind our house in nothing but my underpants and I laugh, laugh out loud, as I run.

A cabin in an apple orchard above Okanagan or Wenatchee. Were we apple pickers then? Lots of asparagus grew in the orchard. They plant it there for a reason that has to do with soil erosion. I gather asparagus in the skirt of my dress for our meals. I love asparagus still. Our neighbors, other apple pickers, are from Oklahoma. They have accents, twangy accents. Mom starts talking like them for the fun of it, but for the rest of her life she will, from time to time, talk with an Okie accent. My mother's friends from Oklahoma take us to their church, where a preacher drives demons out of people in the Name of Our Lord Jesus and very ordinary-looking people talk in tongues and fall down on the floor and otherwise get carried away with the Holy Ghost.

We lived in lots of places. Lots.

The video will end when I am ten because that's when we left our home reservation for good. That is, we would never live there again but would continue to return for visits over the years. Also this is a video of my childhood, and I began to menstruate in August of the year I was ten. My childhood was over, that is, the relatively carefree time before I had to concern myself with bras and Kotex and monthly killer cramps that everyone would tell me were nothing. "You're a woman now," my mother told me. I hated it when she held my new woman status over my head: "What kind of *woman* are you?" (on my lack of neatness, as though I were a disgrace to all women). I didn't ask to be a woman. So what if I were a failure? By my tenth summer all my sisters are married. Mom and Dad and I live in a rather isolated rural area near Tacoma in a comfortable house with two bedrooms and lots of yard space and woods for exploring. Dad has to take the car and go to work every day. Mom can't stand being alone (and just being at home with me, to her, counts as being alone). So Dad drops us off at my middle sister's tiny house very early every morning. The sister I was close to when I was younger, who now has three children of her own and little patience, won't let me in her little house. It has only two rooms. It's just a cabin really. Mom spends all day in there. I can see and hear the TV through the open door. My oldest sister comes to visit sometimes. Sometimes my middle sister's in-laws come around. I stay outside. Anyway there *is* an outhouse. And neighbor kids to play with. I don't really mind that much (except my feelings are hurt that that is my sister's attitude . . . and I resent my mother. We could so easily just be comfortable in our own house, except she can't stand being alone. She'd rather put me through this.), until I begin to bleed. Then I wish I had somewhere to go, a place of my own. A shelter of some kind. I really feel trapped . . . by my own body as well as by circumstance. There is a big woods beyond the grassy fields that stretch out behind my sister's house. I daydream about running away and living out my life in those woods . . . as a wildwoman of the woods.

The video will end with an image of me at ten (in early adolescence . . . people think I am about thirteen) sitting in a woodshed about twenty feet from my middle sister's tiny cabinlike house. The shed has just one wall and a roof. I'm sitting on an old green overstuffed easychair someone must have put there (against the wall) a long time ago, because it's very dirty and smells old and musty. My oldest sister and her children are visiting. I can hear my two sisters and my mother talking and laughing.

My nephew, my oldest sister's oldest child, is climbing a tree beside the shed, hanging upside down by his knees from

a limb. He's seven years old. I'm ten. He's a kid. I'm a
woman. He can swing upside down by his knees. I can
secretly bleed onto a bulky sanitary pad and endure the
pain—worse than a toothache—worse than a sprain or
bruise—worse than anything I'd ever experienced before. I
stoically watch my nephew in the tree.

II

Imagine yourself at the age of thirteen. Your mother decides
she wants to live somewhere else . . . somewhere you have
never been before. This time you and *both* your parents pack
up the car and drive aimlessly from some town on the Washington coast. You drive two hundred miles inland, near the
Coeur d'Alene Reservation where you used to live, then you
drive five hundred miles south. You have no destination in
mind. Finally you come to a town your mother takes a fancy
to: Pocatello, Idaho, in southern Idaho, a region dominated
by the Mormon church. (And Mormons believe that all
brown-skinned people, including American Indians, are
brown because of a sin committed by one of their ancestors.
When God forgives the Lamanites—i.e., people of brown
skin—their complexions will again be white. This will happen sometime in "these latter days." The descendants of
Cain, however, aren't so lucky. They will never be white
again.) Pocatello is an ugly little place surrounded by potato
fields and little else . . . to think you and your parents left the
beautiful Pacific Northwest for this. They rent a little apartment. You settle in. You like your school. You make some

new friends. You don't fit in every place, but you're doing okay in Pocatello. You attend a memorable Halloween party. You're still there for Thanksgiving, but before Christmas your mom decides she hates Pocatello, and you're gone again.

Imagine yourself then at a middle-class high school in Portland, Oregon. Portland, compared with other places you've lived, is relatively urbane and sophisticated. Your mother and your sisters have been telling you how ugly you are most of your life, how strange you are, and nobody has ever said that wasn't true. But suddenly, in Portland, you're attractive. Your whole world has changed. (You're in high school now, but you won't have enough credits for this year to count. This will be your last year.) Attractive girls want to be your friend. Cute boys like you. You've been placed in a special advanced-learning track in Portland, but algebra is giving you some trouble. A cute boy tries to get you to let him come home with you so he can help you with your algebra. You put this boy off. Mostly you don't want him to see your house. You don't want to give your mother a chance to criticize him. Another boy, who is a football player and something of a school celebrity, stops by your locker. He walks you to class sometimes even though you're just a freshman. Your status grows. You even run for class office, but lose. You're just like a teenager in films now, in TV sitcoms. You talk on the phone all the time and you go to the mall and to football games and you attend Catholic Youth Organization events (most of your new friends are of Italian descent). Then the rug gets pulled out from under you again, the high school in Portland vaporizes and you're living in a rural area called Clackamas, Oregon, where nobody seems to find you attractive at all, where you're a nobody again. You hate Clackamas, but you know you won't have to put up with it for long. You know you'll be moving on before long, just like always.

The constant uprooting would have been enough. But then there was also the verbal abuse. I was not normal, she liked to tell me. She mocked the way I walked and talked. She would attack me. Sometimes her attacks came from out of nowhere. Sometimes the smallest thing would set her off.

One night (we lived in Idaho, I know I was five almost six), my half brother and his wife were overnight guests. Mom had my bed, and I had a canvas folding cot. When I got into bed, I found my pillow missing . . . and I had just put it there a little before. "Hey, my pillow is gone. Where is my pillow?" Big mistake. My mother, who had given her pillow to our guests, had taken my pillow for herself.

"Here's your goddamned pillow," she said, throwing it at me. "Here, take it." I knew better than to try to give it back to her. That would only make things worse. The best thing to do now was just keep quiet and hope she wouldn't launch into an attack. No such luck. "I hope you're very comfortable," she said, her voice cracking with emotion. "I hope you remember this night forever. I hope you remember how comfortably you slept with your pillow while I did without. Remember this night when I'm dead and gone, when I'm six feet under." She was almost in tears at this point. I had to be very careful I didn't provoke her further. I shut my eyes and lay very still. Maybe she would think I was asleep.

I was five, almost six, and I was afraid of death. I suspect she knew it, though I never told her. Living on an Indian reservation, you've seen quite a few corpses by the time you're almost six . . . all laid out in their coffins for their wakes and funerals. You've seen the lid shut tight and the coffin carried to the cemetery and lowered into a cold, dark grave, where the dead person must remain alone for all eternity . . . and you've seen the dirt shoveled back into the grave . . . seen it cover the coffin that lay at the bottom. And, living in the country, you've seen a lot of death up close— dead wild animals, carcasses of wild animals or a stray calf . . . in various stages of decomposure, with eyes rotted out of skulls, with ribs exposed. Not to mention dead game. You know absolutely what death is, and if you are a kid like I was, you don't put much stock in that "up in heaven" stuff. Sometimes you obsess about death. Your own. To think your consciousness will come to an end . . . blacked out just like before you were born. Unthinkable. And your parents. They'll die. What will become of you if they die before you grow up?

Dad's appendix ruptured the year I was five. We had to take him seventy miles into Spokane. My youngest sister drove as fast as she could. Luckily the weather was good, no snow blocked the road, no ice or rain made it dangerous. My mother sat up front next to her. Dad lay on the back seat and I sat on the edge of the seat. He had chills and fever. He kept trembling, moaning in pain. We almost didn't make it. But we did. Dad got his ruptured appendix removed, and everything turned out okay in the end. Mom talked about it a lot. Dad's close call . . . about how stubborn he was, how he refused to see the doctor for such a long time. She insisted he draw up a will.

"And don't you come to my funeral," she said that night I'd offended her by asking what had become of my pillow. "I don't want you there. Do you hear me? Answer me."

"Yes." She'd said it before, and she would say it many, many times more.

"I don't want you at my funeral cryin' around, pretendin' you were a normal girl who loved her mother. Just stay the hell away!"

I can overlook the other things she did . . . the hitting and slapping, whipping with a switch she would make me go outside and pick myself . . . things that would be called abuse today don't seem like much. That was what people did in those days. And Mom herself was born just after the turn of the century. To her generation, beating children was considered responsible parenting. If that was all she had done, maybe I would resent it more than I do. Compared to the verbal abuse, though, and the constant uprooting, the whipping and slapping seems like nothing. Just nothing. It is the easiest to understand and forgive.

I've tried to be compassionate as I looked back over my troubled childhood . . . to believe that none of it was her fault. I've tried to believe that it wasn't as bad as I remember. But to look with compassion requires distance and a feeling of safety . . . that you've gone beyond the reach of all that had harmed you way back when.

Mom wasn't depressed. For all her irrational behavior and after all her hard times, and even with the ever-worsening pain of arthritis she must have realized was crippling her more and more as time passed, she was not depressed. She was, for all her meanness, a functioning human being (even later, when she became so horribly crippled, she was always a functioning human being).

But long before she became my mother, before she met my father, she *was* depressed. She described her life to me, how it had been when she was married to her first husband. Not that she had expected much. She wasn't in love or anything. She simply wanted to get away from home. But she hadn't expected it to be the hell it was. What she described to me when I was her little captive confidante I would later recognize as classic symptoms of depression: no will to get out of bed. No involvement in life. She couldn't eat. She couldn't sleep. She had no energy for anything. Sixteen when she married, she spent ten years with this man, during which time she had long periods of torturous depression. In her periods of remission she would contemplate suicide because she had no wish to live through another period of helplessness, when the world looked bleak and hopeless beyond belief.

Then she met my father and she loved someone. At last. She left her first husband and her little son and daughter (she never said how she felt about leaving her daughter, whom she had contact with when the girl grew up, but she often spoke of how it broke her heart to leave her little son. She kept pictures of him in her billfold: one as a toddler, and another as a young veteran going to college on the G.I. Bill. He never forgave her for leaving him. In my whole lifetime she only saw him once, at her own mother's funeral when I was fourteen). She ran away with my dad and she was rather happy, I think, for a time. At very first she drank, like he did. Then soon became a teetotaler and remained one for life.

Then she had my oldest sister . . . the favorite of both of my
parents . . . clearly their favorite . . . I think because she
reminded them both of when they were in love and happy,
before all the messiness, all the sorrow and bad times began.
My father turned out to be (at times) a vicious, brutal drunkard, and he began to beat her when he got drunk . . . for no
reason or for very little reason. Because he was mean and
angry. And Mom was there and couldn't get away from him.
When the other three were small, there was no way she
could take them and get away. She had no place to go. How
would she manage, dragging three kids around? And she
would not abandon another child of hers, not ever again. But
she didn't get depressed.

If Freud were right, if depression is "anger turned inward,
against the self," then Mom wasn't going to make that mistake again. The devil thrived on idleness. Maybe, among
other things, the devil was depression. Mom aggressively
turned her anger, not inward, but outward . . . with great
force . . . away from herself. And I was her safest target
(along with Dad, who had helped create the rage that had
taken root in her soul long ago. Dad was often the victim of
that hateful mouth in later years. Even more, I imagine, after
I was gone).

The anger was there. She'd never had a chance as a child.
She'd had a loveless first marriage to a man who degraded
her, who called her denigrating names . . . who would not
allow music anywhere near him. She'd abandoned two children in order to save her own life. She married for love and
then became victim of her second husband, a battered
woman. With an undependable drunkard for a husband, she
raised three daughters. By the time I knew her, she already

had a wasted life. A lost youth. A crippling illness. The anger was there, and it had to go somewhere. Sometimes, after these attacks, especially if they were particularly dark and violent, she would clear up and her mood would become light. She never expressed any remorse afterward. She acted as though the attacks never happened. The poison was dispelled for the time being. And she never again became the creature she was . . . (the woman she described to me) . . . in her early twenties . . . who, though young and possessing a strong and healthy body, was a human vegetable, a sort of nonperson who lay in bed all day with a dull ache in her heart and stared quietly and unthinking at the walls.

Maybe her running away had something to do with that, too, running . . . on the move, on the road, not tied down. Maybe it gave her a feeling of freedom to be that way. Maybe she felt time running out, her illness creeping ever closer, and she didn't want to just sit still and wait for it to overtake her.

Four years after I left Mom and Dad, they bought a house in Wapato, not fancy but comfortable. It had three bedrooms and a big enclosed porch in back. It could sleep a lot of daughters and sons-in-laws and grandchildren when it had to. Dad fixed it up for her after she became confined to her wheelchair. He had been a carpenter. He was good at that sort of thing. He took the front steps out and put a ramp in their place. He took out a wall in the bathroom and put in sliding doors so she could have access to it. He did quite a bit of remodeling for her. They had a comfortable house (my youngest sister and her husband and six children lived in Wapato). I was nineteen and a mother myself when they bought that house. My father died there. My mother lived there until her final illness. (Except for periods when she lived with my half sister, her oldest daughter, or one of my sisters. A time or two she was gone a year from her own home.)

Once she said to me, when I was in my late twenties, that she and my father had settled in Wapato because of me. And she hated it there . . . had always hated it. They only went there in the first place because of me. She would have preferred Spokane or Tacoma, but she was stuck in Wapato now, old and alone and in a wheelchair. She'd said this before, and I just listened and kept quiet. This time I responded.

"I was sixteen years old when I left Wapato," I said.

"I know," she said, "and it was too late by then for us to go anywhere else. That's what I told him when he said we should stay here for your sake. I told him we had to consider ourselves first. 'She won't stick around Wapato,' I told him. . . . 'Not around us either. She'll be grown and gone before we know it, and here we'll be, holding the bag.' But he insisted. We ended up here, and here I am still to this very day. I always hated it here."

Mom only went to third grade herself, though she was good at reading and writing and arithmetic. She loved school, she said, and I believe it. She wrote much better than many students I've had who were graduating college seniors.

She read books, all kinds of books (except not many novels). But she had no friends or associates who read books. She was, after all, a hotel maid, a nursing-home attendant, a fruit picker, a lower-class housewife. *Playhouse 90* was her favorite

TV program, and of all its productions, *Juno and the Paycock* was her favorite. She loved the movie version of *A Raisin in the Sun*, and she saw the movie version of *The Member of the Wedding* twice. To attend a professional production of a drama was one of her fondest desires (along with seeing Ireland one day). She never got to do either.

What could Mom have done if she'd had a college education, or at least if she'd had a few more years of formal schooling than she did have, if her mother hadn't taken her out of school when she was just nine years old and beginning fourth grade because she needed her at home to help with housework and the care of the little ones?

III

I don't recall where we went after we left Clackamas, Oregon. I do recall I didn't attend school any more that year, though. I had no credits at all in grade nine (but I went and registered myself the following fall at Wapato high school in grade ten. Nobody bothered to find out whether or not I'd gone to school in grade nine). We ended up back in Wapato soon after we left Clackamas.

Back on the Yakima Reservation I felt sophisticated for having lived in Portland. Wapato felt sort of like home to me by now, we'd been back so often. I had friends there that I'd had since I was eleven. Wapato represented a certain continuity. I wasn't sorry to be back.

My youngest sister, who had three daughters by this time,

had bought a beat-up old house in the Horschel Tracks section of Wapato. She was separated from her husband, as she would often be throughout the marriage that would endure some fourteen or so years. My parents and I lived next door to her in a rented house. She worked a lot as a short-order cook, and when the weather got better, in the orchards and fields. My mother was on hand to baby-sit, and my parents, then as always, shared whatever they had with her. My father was completely retired by now, and we lived on Social Security and his army pension and, in the fall, at harvesttime, whatever his wheat land in Idaho made.

That summer, I was fifteen, the owner of our rented house wanted it back. We moved into the storage shack behind my youngest sister's house. The storage shack, set up on cement blocks, had no windows. You could see daylight between the boards that made its walls. The summer, as always in the Yakima Valley, sizzled. I don't know why my parents wanted to stay there. I'm sure they had enough money to rent another house or apartment. But they didn't want to. Not yet.

My parents only used the shack as a sleeping room. Or my mother did. Dad built another, separate room onto its side for his sleeping room. They really lived inside my sister's house. My sister did not allow me in her house. Not ever. Never. Not even to use her toilet.

Her husband returned, and the two of them worked hoeing beets and stripping hops and picking fruit of all kinds as many hours as they could. Sometimes twelve, sometimes more hours. My parents baby-sat and kept house and cooked for them. They had a portable air conditioner, which they took into my sister's house. Mom brought a plate of food out to the shack for me each evening. My father helped my sister's husband build another, large room onto the house. My sister was expecting another baby (she would have seven babies in all before she was done).

I was filled with anger. Hatred towards my sister, the sister who had treated me like so much garbage all of my life . . . and now here I was in her storage shack, enduring the summer, forbidden to enter her house.

But harder to take than my sister's behavior was that of my parents. My parents were supposed to be my parents, weren't they? What did I have if I didn't have them? They were supposed to be interested in my welfare, weren't they? And if they weren't . . . what did that say about me? They allowed her to treat me like that. They condoned it by failing to withdraw their support. Indeed they were the ones who had put me in the position to be mistreated. They let my sister and said nothing to her, went on working for her and helping her, just as they always did, in any way they could.

One of my many theories, devised years later when I looked back on this summer, was that my parents said nothing because of this: My sister had young children, to whom my parents were deeply attached. Maybe this is why they wanted to stay near her . . . to take care of the children. Maybe this is why they did not say a word when she wouldn't let me in her house. Maybe I'm wrong. But that is the theory that is most acceptable to me, far more than that they just didn't care, that I was nothing to them, that I didn't count for anything. It's hard for me to imagine myself in their place and what I would do or say. That was the summer that I began to think I might be a writer someday.

Sitting in that miserable storage shack, I wrote poetry, lots and lots of poetry. At least my sister wasn't getting me out into the fields with her this summer as she had the summer before.

Stripping hops is backbreaking work: dirty and hot and the vines are so sharp you wear out a pair of leather gloves each and every day, first one side and then the other, and the vines whip across your face if you aren't careful (and I didn't know how to be) and leave a long, red welt that stays for a long time and looks like an angry scar.

My sister and her husband were good at this kind of work, very good. But I wasn't. She told my mother the boss complained to her about my work. My rows looked like they hadn't been done, he said. He said I wasn't worth the money he was paying me (which was one dollar an hour . . . eight hours a day, minus two dollars per day for the leather gloves). I wasn't worth six dollars a day. The boss said. Not even worth six dollars a day.

That summer I did no fieldwork. I sat in that shack by myself in the heat and dust and wrote poetry and read James Baldwin novels . . . the first of which, *Go Tell It on the Mountain,* I picked up at the supermarket downtown. Then I read *Giovanni's Room.* Then *Another Country.* No books then about Indians by Indians. I got a collection of Richard Wright's short stories, all of which took place in the Deep South. I was learning so much now. I wrote a great flood of poetry, breaking the dam. I naively sent it to the only publications I knew of that published poetry: *Ingenue* and *Mademoiselle.*

I mailed off a new batch of poems almost every day but didn't include any self-addressed, stamped envelopes like the magazines said. I didn't want them to come back, to fall into the hands of my mother or sister (who had regularly read and ridiculed my early efforts at stories and poems). I didn't even want my new poems back myself. What did I want with them? I knew what they said (though I've quite forgotten now). The important thing was sending them out . . . out and out and out they went . . . out into the world beyond (mailing them was sort of like rolling them up and putting them inside bottles and casting them out to sea) . . . all the way across the continent . . . to New York City. The place where writers live and where books and magazines are published. I didn't expect to be notified that someone was going to publish my work and wanted to pay me . . . but I wouldn't have been surprised if they did. (Nobody did.) It didn't matter.

I began to stay at friends' houses, particularly one, whose father had committed suicide the year before and whose mother, who never drank before that, had begun to drink a lot ever since. This friend and I were very close at this time, and we needed each other that summer. I took to staying at her house almost every night, and my parents, who used to be so strict, so suspicious of me, had nothing to say about it.

I stayed out all night with my pals (not all of whom were poor, even though they were all Indians), my old gang back in Wapato. We went swimming every day. We rode horses. We drove up to the cool mountains. Once we drank beer (which I was the actual buyer of, disguised as an adult in high-heel shoes and makeup and my hair in a French twist. I had gone into six different taverns trying to "score." At the last one the bartender didn't even look at me. He was watching TV. And it was dark in there). We lay in the shade eating chips and drinking Cokes and listening to popular songs on the radio and on the 45-rpm record player. "Green Onions," was really big and "The Lion Sleeps Tonight" and

"Splish, Splash." And I read novels about black people and wrote miles and miles of poetry about God only knows what and fantasized about one day being a writer, a real writer. That would be my last summer at home.

IV

When I grew up, I lived in California. For a short time in '83 I lived in beautiful Vancouver, British Columbia. (The Jay Treaty of 1794 grants what amounts to dual citizenship to "Native North American Indians" in recognition of the fact that white people were imposing an artificial dividing line in Indian country. Some tribes that lived along the border would have been divided in half by the international border were it not for the Jay Treaty.)

My mother's mother belonged to one of those border tribes, the Kootenay, which is made up of five bands. The Kootenay remain in their ancestral land, but, because of the borders, three bands are in the Canadian province of British Columbia, one in the state of Idaho, and the other in Montana. My mother (who was never an enrolled member of her mother's tribe because her father, to whom her mother was legally married, was a white man. It used to work that way in Canada until 1986.) was born in a little town that no longer exists near Cranbrook, British Columbia, in Kootenay country. I've known many Canadian Indians who came to the United States to live and work and returned to Canada when and if it suited them. It was my intention, when I finished my master's degree in English in California, to make

Vancouver my home. It felt like home to me in a way California never did. The Pacific Northwest. Snow-capped mountains. Evergreen trees. Lovely rain, rain, rain. Native Indians. Home. I had reached my mid-thirties by then, my second marriage was over. I wanted to go home. As the granddaughter of a Kootenay woman and the great-great-granddaughter of a Kootenay chief, I had deep roots in British Columbia, deeper than any non-Indian person.

I loved Vancouver. It had the look and feel of home but without the ghosts of the past—without sisters and nieces and nephews and Indians at every turn who knew one of them or some or all of them. I could live in Vancouver, or so I thought, as part of an Indian community. I could have a place where I belonged. And I could be free at the same time, really free of the names and faces of those closest to me who had treated me so badly when I was growing up. Home at last. Only it wasn't to be.

The Jay Treaty turned out to be a one-way street, and I was going the wrong way. The United States honors it. Canada does not. The Canadian government believes the Jay Treaty is not an agreement between Canada and the United States but between the United States and Great Britain. Canada is not bound by it. Canada, my new home, had no room for me. No room for a lot of people. One illegal alien in the news when I was there was a pregnant woman from war-torn El Salvador. She petitioned Immigration to regard her unborn child as a Canadian citizen, since it was conceived in Canada. But the woman, who was a big-bellied seven months gone, was deported back to El Salvador.

I could have applied for citizenship of course. That was a long way around and it would require me to "renounce" the country of my birth. My country. The United States of America.

Dad used to play a silly game with me when I was little: I would hear "The Star-spangled Banner" playing on the radio (he would turn it up loud) before a ball game. That was the signal. I'd come running. There he would be, standing at attention beside the radio, eyes straight ahead, right hand over his heart. I would pick my father's pockets as the band played and someone sang the national anthem. (He would have filled his pockets with coins ahead of time.) "Oh, my God!" he would cry in mock terror. "Someone is picking my pockets!" I would laugh as I picked. "And I can't do a thing about it because I'm so patriotic!" He was so patriotic, he had to stand still while I robbed him. I had to work quickly. I had to be finished and out the door before the song ended. I always made it. I would be hiding somewhere counting my money and giggling as the last words rang out, "the la-a-and of the freeeeeeeeee. And the home . . . of the braaaave!"

Could the daughter of a man that patriotic renounce her country? I don't think so. Dual citizenship is one thing. Renouncing one's country is quite another.

In the fall of 1983, almost flat broke, I took a job as instructor of English at Northwest Indian College on the Lummi Indian Reservation just south of the border in Bellingham, Washington. I felt nervous returning to Washington State (even though I'd never been to Bellingham before)—the scene of so much heartache. But I did. I went back. And it was all right.

In 1985 I accept a one-year appointment at the University of Washington in Seattle as Distinguished Visiting Writer, thus moving closer to my beginnings.

Seattle is familiar terrain. One sister and all her grown children still live in the area and some of the grown children of another. Here I am—going on forty now—but in my soul's darkest corner I am ever the motherless child, the psychologically tortured girl I used to be, the scapegoat of my troubled, troubled family. Seattle makes it all come alive again, fills my dreams, my waking moments too. I don't feel like any "distinguished writer." I feel like someone who has something wrong with them . . . very seriously wrong, intrinsically wrong. Sometimes it's hard for me to function in Seattle. I wake at four A.M. and can't go back to sleep. The city is grey. Hell on hills. The rain comes pouring down (and is no longer lovely at all) every day. I remember what my mother used to tell me: no matter what you do or where you go, you can't get away from what you really are.

My mother lives very near me now, with my middle sister in Tacoma. The girl who was, perhaps, the most beloved of my mother's grandchildren, my youngest sister's eldest daughter, became my mother's caretaker. This niece, a very young mother on her own when she went to live in my mother's house and take over her full-time care, once told me Gram was the one person in her life she knew she could depend on come what may, who never failed her. Gram was her rock. They always got along. They understood each other. And, she insisted, Gram was not a burden to her, her Gram who had so lovingly cared for her when she was a baby and little girl. Taking care of Gram, however, wasn't an easy task. She had to be fed and bathed, her medicines carefully administered, and she had to be turned very, very carefully from one side to the other. Between Gram and her children, my niece had little time. Gram wanted her to do something for herself, to prepare for her future, and they came up with a scheme. Once all my niece's children were in school, they hired a nurse's aid to come in several days a week and my niece took out some loans and enrolled in a course of study at a community college. I think she wanted to be a physician's assistant. She told me my mother's doctor told her she would make a good one. My mother was so fragile. My niece, who was strong and gentle, knew just exactly how to turn my mother, but the nurse's aide was less skilled, and one day while my niece was at school, the aide turned my mother and my mother's hip fractured. My niece had to drop out of school. My mother, despite her age and condition, fully recovered from the fracture over time. Eight years passed. Mom had illnesses that required hospitalization and convalescence in a nursing home. A time or two one of her daughters cared for her in their homes. But mostly, for eight long years, it was this granddaughter who cared for her night and day, bathed her, fed her, combed her hair, turned her in bed. Made sure my mother did not succeed in tricking other people into giving her things she wasn't supposed to have. (She once got me to make her some coffee. I was carrying it to her when my niece woke up and stopped me. Mom wasn't supposed to have coffee.)

My mother became seriously ill and had to be hospitalized and then had to spend months convalescing in a nursing home. My niece and her children visited her often there, but my niece's energy was drained. She couldn't care for my mother on a full-time basis anymore. She was too tired. She couldn't. That was how it happened, then, that when my mother was released from the nursing home, she did not return at first to her own home in Wapato. She went to Tacoma, where my middle sister takes care of her now.

I decide to visit Mom in the late summer of 1985.

I drive very fast. It takes me less than forty-five minutes to get from my apartment in Seattle to my sister's in Tacoma.

I am shocked when I see my mother. I am always shocked, even though she's looked like this for years. I forget. She doesn't look this way in my memories, in my dreams. I never think of her this way.

V

My mother, who weighed more than two hundred pounds while I was growing up, is now a tiny, emaciated skeleton of a woman, just eighty-three pounds. Her hands were, for a while, closed into tight fists. Now, after physical therapy, they are drawn into claws instead. She can move her fingers a little, not enough to feed herself or comb her hair, though. She uses her fingers to sort of "wave" a greeting or a good-bye. Her arms are permanently bent, held close to her body. The joints of her elbows, the largest part of her thin arms, jut out sharply beneath thin, dry skin. Her knees, too, are bent, but not as much as before the therapy. Her legs don't lie flat. She can't turn her head from side to side, even, because of arthritis in her neck. She must be turned from one side to the other every three or four hours. Getting turned is excruciatingly painful for her, but it must be done. I don't understand quite why.

She has lupus, too, and ailments of old age and conditions

caused by her arthritis (such as the ulcers caused by all the aspirin that she must take . . . and sometimes the ulcers bleed, and then she is anemic) and by her forced sedentariness.

Her eyesight is so poor, she can no longer make out the images on the TV screen (though her hearing is still good). The television is always on. It keeps her company. She holds the remote control. One thing she can do with her fingers now that therapy has released them from the closed fist is hold the remote and change the channels.

They keep the window blinds down in the room because her eyes are sensitive to light (even though she wears dark glasses). The window is closed, the room is overheated. She is always cold.

If I found myself in this condition, I would have a hard time believing in God. She doesn't. But then, her God was always a cruel and punishing God and He always did work in strange ways. Here, in her room in my sister's house, there is no crucifix on the wall, no statue of the Virgin Mary (as there is in her own home).

My sister, who has just prepared my mother's meal, is used to seeing her this way, but taking care of our mom is a lot of work. Washington State has a "respite care" program to give the full-time caretakers of invalids a needed break (so that they will be less likely to run out of gas). But nobody in our family applies for respite care anymore. Mom doesn't like the respite people. They act stupid, she says. Some of them can't speak English. She doesn't trust them. She doesn't want them around.

Mom isn't surprised to see me. She seems mildly pleased. She comments on my sunglasses. Do they provide protection

from the glare of sunlight? Is that what they're supposed to
do? (Her eyesight seems pretty good to me.) I admit they are
mostly for decoration. "Decoration, hummmph!" she scoffs.
They're rose-tinted. I'm trying to look at the world through
rose-tinted lenses. She asks me how much I weigh now.
When I tell her I'd rather not say, she says, "I don't wonder." I offer to feed her her meal, and my sister hands me
the plate. I sit in the chair beside my mother's bed and feed
her. My sister leaves the room and is back in a few minutes
with another chair and an iced soft drink. If I don't mind, she
says, she has an errand to run. When she finishes her drink.
If I could stay with Mom for an hour or so. I tell her, Sure,
I don't mind. Mom eats very little. Feeding her doesn't take
long.

My mother's voice is so weak, weaker some days than
others. Today she sounds very weak. She begins telling me
how mean her mother and sisters were to her when she was
young. They mocked her, she says, the way she walked
. . . the way she talked. (I never heard her say this before. I
wonder if this is true, or if she got mixed up and began to
think what she'd done to me was done to her instead.) They
treated her so badly, she says . . . why? Why did they do it?

I put my arm around her shoulders (sort of, as best I can
without hurting her) and try to comfort her. "Just don't think
about it," I tell her.

"I can't help it," she says, "I can't get it out of my mind.
Why were they so mean? Why were they like that? Sometimes I lay awake at night thinking, remembering." Her eyes
well with tears.

"It's all over now. All that stuff is in the past," I tell her,
"Don't think about it anymore." She sheds a tear (which she

cannot wipe away herself. I wipe it away.). She has nothing
to distract her . . . except for visitors. She can't read anymore. She can listen to TV and she can change the channels.
That's all. Nothing to get her away from her ruminations.

Yet I, too, have lain awake, comparatively young and
healthy as I am, with lots of distractions. I ask myself why
too. Why did they do those things? Why did they—with
Mom as their leader—excommunicate me from the family?

Confronting my mother was always out of the question. It
was ridiculous even to consider doing it now with her in this
condition. What if I asked her, "What about yourself, Mom?
You talk about how mean they were to you . . . what about
the way you treated me? Do you remember how you used
to send me out of the house every morning in tears? Do you
recall, at all, those venomous early-morning attacks? How
you would nag me as I got myself ready for school: 'Look at
you. You make me sick the way you primp and preen in
front of the mirror as if you were a pretty girl. Get that idea
out of your head. Look at me when I'm talking to you. Look
at me, damn you. You're not pretty. You're not. You're not
anything!' "

*One morning, when I was in the seventh or eighth grade (I don't
remember if it really was just one morning, though. Maybe it was
something she did over and over again, a routine. But it is burned into
my memory as "one morning."), just as I was about to make my escape,
she woke up and called me back. "You get back here right now!" I went
back.*

*"Don't think you can get away from what you are by getting away
from me!" She hadn't put her dentures in yet. Her mouth looked ugly*

*and loose. She was going full throttle. "You think you can walk out of
here . . . go to that damned dumb school and be somebody else, don't
you. Well, you can't. You can't fool anybody, no matter how "nice" you
act . . . no matter how much you smile (and she mocked me here, how
I looked smiling and simpering and trying to act nice. The effect was
grotesque.) and put on a show. It won't work. People will instinctively
know what an evil thing you are. They'll draw away from you in
revulsion"— and here she acted this part out, too, the innocent, confused
expressions on the faces of the people as they draw away from me— "and
they'll say, 'There's something about that girl. Something not quite right.
It gives you a bad feeling to be around her.' Nobody will ever want to
be around you for long. Nobody decent. Now go. Get the hell out of here.
Get the hell out of my sight!"*

She was a master, an absolute master, of verbal abuse.
Nothing she ever told me that her own mother did or said,
and she'd told me plenty during those years when I was her
forced confidante, could hold a candle to her repertoire.

Most of the time I did manage to escape the early-morning attacks. I spent a lot of mornings hanging around school
buildings waiting for them to be unlocked and opened up. In
winter I would wait in the early-morning dark and cold. One
winter morning I waited until it was full daylight, and not
one bus had arrived and no one had come to raise the flag.
Finally I realized I had come to school on a Saturday.

But I comfort her now in her illness and helpless old age
as she tells me of the cruelty inflicted upon her that she
cannot forget. She sheds a tear or two for herself. I wipe
them away.

. . . .

I remember another summer day in this same city twenty-eight years before. We three were all there that day, too, back in 1957: my mother, my middle sister (whose house we are now in) and me. I was eleven years old at the time, this sister was twenty-three, and Mom was fifty-four and still going strong.

Mom and Dad and I lived in Tacoma at the time in a cheap house in a poor, rundown, black neighborhood. (Mom took me and left him at the end of that summer, and we went to Wapato for the first time.). When we lived in that house, I had my own bedroom.

My bedroom was directly above the living room, and I often spied on the goings-on in the living room through the heat vent in the floor.

The day I recall is July 4, 1957. My mother and three adult sisters, their husbands, and already by this time many, many children have been planning an all-day picnic at Lake Tapps. My father had to work that day, and since it was a holiday, Mom knew in advance that he would go to a tavern after work and "get tanked up." She wants to be gone when he gets home. He's already ruined enough holidays to last her a lifetime. (He was sixty-five then but still worked full eight-hour days in the blazing sun.)

Mom told me weeks before that I could not go to Lake Tapps on the Fourth. She didn't want me along spoiling things.

She was still strong, though she had bad days when arthritis prevented her from using her hands much. Sometimes her knees ached, and she complained of pain in her shoulders a lot. But she wasn't crippled yet. She hadn't begun to waste away. She still looked fierce and intimidating when she stood in my room shaking her fist, swearing at me and telling me what I had to do.

That's what she did one day weeks before the Fourth of July when she told me I wasn't to be included in the picnic plans: "and don't you try to pull anything either. Don't you dare. Nobody wants you around. Nobody. They might say they do just to be polite to me because I'm your mother, but they really don't. If anyone should ask you why you're not coming, you tell them you don't feel like it. Understand? Don't say one word . . . not one word about how Mom said you can't come along!"

On the Fourth they all gather at my parents' home, packing their cars, making last-minute arrangements. I am so angry. Full of rage. I feel it boiling inside of me. I go up to my room and lie on my bed. And weep. Then I go to the heat vent and carefully, quietly, open the grill and lie on my stomach on the floor.

My mother sits on a big easy chair directly below the vent. Her hair is grey, but she dyes it auburn. It is parted in the middle, and from my vantage point I can plainly see the regrowth at the roots.

I can't see my middle sister, but I can hear her voice. Not as clearly as I can hear my mother, though. They've been talking about me. She's asking Mom why I'm not going to the lake with them.

"I don't know," Mom says, "she just said she doesn't want to go. That's all I know." My mother's tone is light, as though she were resigned to my "kids will be kids" behavior.

"She didn't say why? What's the matter with her?"

"No. She didn't say why."

"She can't stay here alone. She's just a kid."

"Far be it from me to force a person to do something against their will," Mom says. Hah. "She'll be all right. Don't worry about her. I'm going to leave her some hot dogs to heat up. She can watch TV. You know she likes to be alone."

"I'm going to tell her she must come with us."

"Well." Mom gestures: She raises her hands and shoulders in a shrug, as if it were all a matter of indifference to her. The liar. The old liar. It doesn't occur to me then, but it will years later that she probably lied about me to my sisters a lot. About what I said and why I did things. She needed them to be on her side against me. But that day I just think, There's my proof that she lies. From then on whatever she says will be suspect to me. I will never simply believe her again. Anything she says may or may not be a lie. From then on she will have less power over me because I know she lies. "Go ahead," she tells my middle sister. "But you're just wasting your time. She's not going to change her mind." Mother knows best.

Mom is so sure of herself. She thinks she has me wrapped around her finger, that I dare not disobey her. Would anyone believe me if I did expose her? Would anyone care? "Come on, you'll have a good time. Why do you want to stick around here all day by yourself? You can swim. There'll be lots of people there." No. No, no, no. I don't want to go. At that point I don't. How would I manage it feeling such rage as I do towards my mother?

Before they leave, Mom calls me downstairs to tell me she is leaving a box of sparklers for me. Such a thoughtful mother. They are in the drawer of the telephone stand. I resolve not to eat the hot dogs. I will not light those stupid sparklers either. I will punish her for what she's doing.

About midnight, though, the hunger gets to be too much, and I end up eating. No pride. No pride at all. I take the stupid box of sparklers out on the front porch and sit there in the dark and light them up one by one.

I look into the white light of the sparks and concentrate all of my anger, all of the hatred I am feeling into the center of the light:

Someday I'll run away. Soon. Far, far away and I will never see them or their damned faces again or hear their damned voices. I will become rich and famous and powerful. They'll come crawling to me. But it won't do them any good because I'm not going to be a wimp like Cinderella or the Ugly Duckling or Joseph (of the coat of many colors), who forgave their tormentors. No. I won't. Let them crawl. Let them beg. They won't get anything from this girl. They can go to hell.

When the sparklers are all burned out, I sit alone in the dark. My father drives up and stumbles out of his car and up the front steps. Still in his dirty white carpenter pants. He collapses onto the rocking chair on the porch and passes out; his head lolls forward, his chin on his chest. I can't leave him here. I sit with him until the merry gang of celebrators arrive home.

My mother smiles and her face is flushed. I can see she has had a very good time. One of my brothers-in-law helps my father upstairs and puts him to bed.

.   .   .

Twenty-eight years later, in the home of the same sister who
tried to coax me along on that Fourth of July, I comfort my
aged, hideously crippled mother as she tells me she is
haunted by memories of how badly her mother and sisters
mistreated her. (She was not the youngest. She was two years
younger than one sister and older than the others. She
couldn't have been as defenseless against them as I was
against her and my sisters.) She is so old and sick, frail, pitiful
beyond words.

A few nights after my visit I have a dream that will recur
over the next year and a half:

*My mother and I are alone in a house that is old and poorly furnished.
It is neat and tidy, the way she always kept the places she lived. She
must be cooking, boiling something, because the windows are all fogged
over. Therefore all that can be seen through the windows is grey light.
My father is outside sitting in a car in the driveway beside the house,
warming up the engine of the car. It is winter in this dream. My mother
is not crippled as she is in real life, but she is old, tiny, withered. I am
not a child. I am myself as I really am. She lies down on a single bed
that is neatly made. I am entering middle age and I am twice her size,
yet it does not seem odd to me that I am eager to lie down with her (like
I used to be when I would give my sisters the slip and sneak into the
room where she lay sleeping when I was little and she worked at the
apple dryer). She doesn't seem surprised when I lie down with her. I try
to snuggle close to her, but she is so small. I want to be held in her arms.
I want to feel safe in her arms.*

*Then my father comes in the door from outside and says he's ready.
Mom gets up, puts on her coat, picks up her pocketbook. It doesn't seem
odd that she, who was eleven years younger than Dad in real life, is now
much older.*

I think we are all going somewhere in the car and I try to follow them out the door, but they won't let me. "You have to stay here," my father tells me in his stern voice.

I beg them not to leave me: "Don't leave me. Please. Take me with you. Mom? Mamma?"

"You aren't coming. That's all there is to it," she says.

As the dream ends, I am standing inside the house at the front door, which has a glass window in its upper half. I wipe the steam off the glass to make a space to look through. I watch my parents get in the car and drive down a long, bumpy dirt road to a highway beyond. (It appears as though the house I am in is isolated, out in the country. I don't see any other houses.) My parents don't look back. I feel like my heart is breaking.

I visit my mother at my sister's house in Tacoma one more time a few weeks later. She and my sister are leaving Tacoma now, going back to my mother's house in Wapato. I don't understand why. Just my sister and Mom. My sister, then, all alone, will be Mom's caretaker. She doesn't know how long it will be. Maybe forever.

I spend a weekend in Wapato and give my sister a break. The others and some of the grandchildren, too, come for visits. My sister can get away then. But mostly, she is very restless. She says she feels like the Prisoner of Zenda. She keeps remembering, she says, the day Mom came to the TB facility in Idaho. My sister was a poor sick little girl then, Mom's sick little girl, who had been pining for home. No one, it seemed, ever came home from that place. They just stayed there until they died. Mom said later she'd had a dream that my sister had died and she had to come and get her.

The doctors had refused to let her go, would not give my mother my sister's clothes. They talked to her like she was some dumb little woman. "If you take her out of here she'll die," they told her. "You might as well just hold a gun to your daughter's head and pull the trigger." Mom didn't try to argue with them. Mom didn't care what they said. She was taking her child home. My sister was in a nightgown and slippers, and this was winter in Idaho. Mom took off her own coat and put it on my sister and, taking her by the hand, headed for the door. The doctors gave back my sister's clothes and let her go. Mom took her home. Mom was a hero that day. My sister was the happiest little girl in the world. She was sure then and she's still sure Mom saved her life that day. She took her home. Took care of her herself. Did some research and decided what to do. Took her to the sanitarium in Tacoma. My sister remembers all that. Still, in Wapato, she feels like the Prisoner of Zenda and the days pass slowly.

Then my niece comes to visit, the one who was my mother's caretaker for such a long time before. She isn't tired anymore. She can do it again, she says. She wants to do it. She has missed her Gram. The old order is restored. My sister returns to Tacoma. My niece is once again my mother's caretaker. Her children once again make crayon drawings for Mom, which they tape to her bedroom wall, and read to her from their schoolbooks and tell her about their days. My niece and my mother together again.

VI

The call I am expecting never comes. One day in March of 1987 I call my mother's house and her granddaughter-care-taker tells me my mother was admitted to the hospital the day before and is not expected to live. The doctor said anyone who wants to see her should come now. My niece already called her mother and my other two sisters, and they are on their way to Wapato.

"Why didn't you call me?" Dead silence.

"I was *going* to call you," my niece says. "I just didn't get around to it yet." She sounds irritated.

I have a feeling, though, that Mom probably instructed her not to notify me when her death was imminent. She always said, after all, when I was a child, that she didn't want me at her funeral. Maybe she didn't want me at her deathbed either. I can imagine her, even, lying in her frozen position, remembering me as an awful child. Nothing to distract her. All her memories of me. What a bad little girl. Such an ingrate. I undermined all her efforts. The thoughts go round and round. If someone is there, she will share them with that person:

I worked so hard curling her hair, trying to make her look decent for school. Then I happened to look out the window one morning right after she left, and there she was, hiding in the alley, messing up her hair with both hands, trying to pull out the curls I'd worked so hard to make. I vowed then and there I'd never lift a finger to do anything for her again.

That was one of her favorite stories. She repeated it over and over again as the years went by. It was interesting to me that Mom cherished that story for what it said to her concerning my intrinsic bad character. It is an important incident to me, too, because it shows me at the age of just six, unable to openly resist my mother's dictates, but not bending to her will, either, when it went against my best interests. Just six years old, but there I was, hiding, undoing what my mother had done to me before stepping out into the world. (And, to me, those curls were ridiculous. I felt like a damned fool in those Shirley Temple curls.) She quit curling my hair after that day she happened to see me taking some control over my life. But she wouldn't let me wear it just straight the way I wanted. She cut it off instead, all of it, almost like a crew cut, so short she used my father's electric clippers on the back of my neck. I knew I was being punished for defying her. I hated that short haircut, but not half as much as I hated the curls.

Maybe she hadn't instructed my niece not to notify me. Maybe she really just hadn't gotten around to calling me. Whether or not Mom had left instructions that I wasn't to be notified wasn't really relevant, since I knew I had to go to her.

It happened that I suffered a very serious illness in late 1986 that I hadn't recovered from yet. I support myself very meagerly on royalties from past publications and on honorariums for lectures and literary readings. In a few days I will begin a lecture tour that will have to support me all through that spring and summer. I must conserve my strength and my limited energy. My car is old. I am alone. Still, not going to Wapato is out of the question. Out of the question. It involves a six-hour drive.

· · · ·

Chinook, the shortest, most spectacular and most dangerous route is not yet open. Snoqualmie Pass, the long way around, is the route I take. Up, into the mountains I go in my little silver Plymouth Arrow. In March even sedate Snoqualmie is spectacular and dramatic as the ice and snow of winter begins to melt. But no ice or snow blocks the road. The road is clear. The car radio does not work in the mountains. The silence is intense. I wonder if my mother will still be alive when I get there.

My mother took care of me when I was sick. I was sick an awful lot: mumps, measles, chicken pox, all the usual. And sometimes the exotic: hepatitis, scarlet fever, strep throat, some that were never diagnosed because she didn't take me to the doctor. I had such high fevers sometimes when I was sick, I would lose my mind in delirious dreams so beautiful I would hate to come back from them. One was like the world of the animated Disney film *Peter Pan*. Batman was another. I was Batman's friend and helper. He and I were down by the river hiding in the weeds from villains. He didn't have a gun. My mother put cold cloths on my forehead.

"Mom, do you have Batman's gun?"

"No, I don't." She put an aspirin in my mouth, held my head up, made me swallow some water to wash it down.

"Give it back to him, Mom. Batman needs his gun."

She used to read to me when I was sick. Sometimes, if I was very sick, she would stay up all night reading to me. She read all of the Brothers Grimm and Hans Christian Andersen. Once, when we had no storybook in the house, she read to me from a book she'd brought home from the library for herself. It was about Admiral Byrd's explorations in Antarctica. I don't recall what she read, but I recall the pictures that formed in my mind of the little penguins cavorting in the snow.

Will she be there, my mom, when I arrive? Or is she gone already? The day is so dim.

Mom doesn't recognize me when I arrive. She is, of course, very, very ill, trembling in pain, her entire body shaking. Her face is grey. Nothing will save her, the doctor says, but a transfusion will make her remaining time more comfortable. She seems afraid of me. "Who are you?" she asks breathlessly. It's hard for her to speak. "What do you want?"

"What do you expect?" my oldest niece asks. "You never come to see her. Why should she know you? How long has it been?" She's no kid. At thirty-five she is just five years younger than I. I ignore her. She keeps asking me how long it's been since I last visited my mother. Keeps saying how can I expect her to recognize me. I keep ignoring her.

My niece sees a *New Woman* magazine on the stand beside my mother's bed. "Is that yours, Gram? Are you going to be a new woman?" My mother knows my niece is talking to her, is asking her a question, but she doesn't get it.

"What . . . did . . . you . . . say?" Her voice is faint. Mom thinks she's asking a serious question and she struggles to understand, to grasp it. My niece giggles.

My two older sisters sit laughing and visiting in my mother's room in intensive care.

I want to yell at them: "Stop laughing. Get out of here if you want to laugh, you hyenas! And you, you condescending ass, stop asking my mother if that's her magazine and if she's going to be a new woman. Get out. All of you. She's in pain. She's dying. Leave her in peace!" But I don't have a right to say anything like that nor to kick anyone out of Mom's room. All of my sisters have put in long stints as Mom's caretaker. I would relieve them once in a while when I came to visit. Once I gave her a sponge bath. I stayed with her the summer after Dad died when she was in a wheelchair but wasn't so badly off, could still do most things for herself. I've stayed away a lot. Compared to my sisters, I've done very little. If anyone doesn't belong here, it's me, not them. I'm the one who will go away.

I drive around aimlessly. This is the place we returned to most often in those running-away years, then the place where I "came home" to visit my parents. All these years. But it isn't home. No ancestral link to this place. No blood ties. Yakima Indian land. Not home.

I feel nervous, agitated. Going back to my hotel is out of the question. I would pace in my hotel room. I drive past the old movie theater. The Last Picture Show, as it were. That's where I had my first date. I even remember the film: *Village of the Damned.* The boy was from White Swan. The handsomest boy . . . I heard he moved to Seattle and became a hairdresser. The movie theater is a video store now.

I remember the first time we came here, Mom and I: One night I am sick. Mom and I are at my youngest sister's shack. (I am eleven, so my sister is twenty-one.) She has only one child and is pregnant with her second. Her husband is gone. Maybe he's away working.

My mother and I are in bed on the floor. I am coughing.

I can't stop. My sister's voice like thunder in the darkness: "Stop that coughing or I will throw you out. I mean it. If I hear one more sound out of you, out you go!" In the night . . . into the street . . . with no clothes but the T-shirt and underpants I am wearing. It was the sort of thing she would do. I hold both hands over my mouth. I put my head under a pillow.

Early the next morning she tells Mom she doesn't have to go. Just me. "You don't have to go, Mom. I just don't want that thing in my house anymore!" But Mom does leave with me, looking very put out and long-suffering.

Oh, it is so hot. Blistering. It hurts to breathe the air it is so hot and dry. I have a sore throat, a pounding headache. A fever. I feel weak.

We finally come to the park near the old movie theater and the U.S. Café. I lie on the grass in the shade. The green grass is cool, so cool against my face. I can stay there forever.

My mother leaves me to find a pay phone to try to call my father. Miraculously she is able to reach him right away. He's coming for us, she tells me, but won't be there until that evening, until well after dark. My mother and I spend the whole day in the park waiting. The time passes quickly for me. I just lie on the grass and rest in the cool shade.

I think maybe I was sort of my mother's sacrifice. Allowing my sisters to abuse me was part of what bought her way into their lives. And, of course, I was her own scapegoat.

When I was in my first year of college in San Francisco, I wrote a letter to Mom (I was taking Social Psychology 101) telling her I'd learned that *all* families have a member they use as a scapegoat. (I think my youngest sister was their scapegoat before I was born, and when I came along, they shifted it onto me, but not all of it . . . she remained their partial scapegoat too. The youngest of the three, the one who threw me out when I was eleven years old and very sick, took to her role as persecutor with zeal.)

It was reassuring to me to learn that other families scape-goated their children, certain of their children. I thought telling my mother would make her feel better . . . as if she felt bad about what she'd always done, as if she thought about it at all. Maybe my motive was not as simple as that, though. Maybe I was also hoping that if I wrote Mom and told her all about this family-scapegoat stuff I'd learned about, she would have to acknowledge what she'd done. She would be forced to think about it then and express some remorse. But that wasn't her way. Forever after, Mom would say she "read somewhere" that every family has a scapegoat . . . and in our family . . . *she was it!*

Mom had believed she was our family's scapegoat long before I wrote that letter telling her what I'd learned in college. I don't recall her ever telling my sisters anything like that, but she would tell me, when she was all wound up, "bawling me out." Then she would refer to us collectively, sometimes, as "this damned outfit." She would say all fami-lies she had ever known or ever heard of treated their moth-ers with great love and respect, all but "this damned outfit! I've never seen anything like it!"

The next evening I return to the hospital. Mom is feeling much better now. She has had a transfusion and she's rested. She *looks* much better, but, the doctor warns, she isn't. She's dying.

She knows me now, but she keeps getting confused as to

the date (the year, I mean, or the era) and the place. I am given permission to spend the night in her room on a little fold-out cot. My middle sister had spent the night before and one of my nieces the night before that. Someone will be with her every night. She always hated to be alone.

She looks much more than just "better" that evening. She looks refreshed. She looks happy, happier than I've seen her in a long, long while. My own spirits are lifted. She smiles. A nurse comes in and asks her if she wants her pain pill, and she nods yes, and the nurse gives it to her, then a drink of water to swallow it. "Has she been taking pain medication?" The nurse says yes. I am surprised, even under the circumstances. My mother didn't believe in taking drugs.

Nearly twenty years before, when my father died, my sisters called my parents' family doctor and told him Mom was having a hard time and asked him if he could prescribe some tranquilizers or something for her. He came to the house.

Mom was angry at them for calling the doctor and angry at him for giving her a bottle of tranquilizers and trying to get her to take some.

"Do you think you'll become addicted?" the doctor, who was young enough to be her son, asked Mom in a kind but condescending tone. "Is that what you're afraid of? Don't worry, you won't get addicted. You're going through a rough time just now. This is just some medication to help you through your hard time."

"Of course I'm having a hard time!" my mother told the doctor. "I just saw my husband of forty years die. I sat here in this room and watched him die. And today I'm going to bury him! Yes, I'm having a 'hard time.' I'm supposed to be having a 'hard time.' " You could always hear her quotation marks. "It's something I have to go through, and I don't need any damned pills to 'help me.' " The doctor left the pills "just in case." She didn't take any. That's the way she was about such things. Now, though, she has consented to powerful, narcotic painkillers. That's why she's feeling so much better.

Mom tells me that her father came to visit her that day. Her dear father! They had a really good visit, a good time. She was so happy to see him. He was still the same old Dad she knew, making jokes, teasing her. It was wonderful to see him. Then her older sister (by a year or two, my mother was the second oldest), Annie, with whom she never got along, dropped by for a little while. Still the same old Annie too. Mom was glad she didn't stay long. And, she says, she had seen my father too.

"Dad? You saw Dad? He was here?"

"No. Not here. I saw him. At the other end." She's so economical with her words. Conserving her energy.

"End of what, Mom?"

"At the other end of the tunnel. He motioned to me with his arm. He called to me, 'Maaargaret! Maaargaret! Come on, hurry up. Hurry!' I told him I wasn't ready. He's just going to have to wait. Now he's mad."

"He's mad?" She nods yes.

"You remember how he looked, the look he got when he had a mad on." Yes, I remember.

"He got that look. Then he folded his arms over his chest and turned back. He's still there, waiting for me at the other end of the tunnel, his back turned." My mother laughs. "Of course," she says, "I know I'm probably just imagining all this. Probably it's the medication they gave me. Maybe that's it. But it was so nice to see my dad again. I was so happy." Her father had died fourteen years before I was born.

Sometimes Mom's back in Idaho. Sometimes she's a young wife again. It seems she was happy with my father in the beginning.

Sometimes we're in California and I haven't been born yet. I tell her, then, that that was forty years ago. I was born. Here I am.

"That was an awful labor. The worst one. And the worst pregnancy."

"I know, Mom. You told me before."

She sleeps and wakes again. She seems to be in a lot of pain, and again accepts the pain medication and seems all right.

Four nurses, two on each side of her bed, two male and two female, come to turn her at hourly intervals. They are desensitized, of course, but I'm not. Her suffering is too intense to bear, as if all the suffering of all her years is concentrated into those several minutes it takes them to turn her little body from one side to the other: "Oh, God," she screams, "No! Please don't! Please! Please!"

Finally I go to the nurses' station and ask them to stop doing this. It's torture to her, and the doctor said she's dying. Can't they just let her die in peace?

"All right," I'm told, "We won't turn her anymore if that is your wish."

"It is."

"Do you know why we turn her? To keep her lungs from filling with fluid. If we don't keep turning her, that's what will happen. She'll drown in her own fluids. Is that what you

want?" No. Of course it isn't. They continue turning her
every hour or so. Each time she screams in pain and begs
them to stop. "Oh, God," she calls. *God.* I wonder if she's
had last rites, if anyone thought of it.

At the nurses' station they check and tell me yes. A priest
came to her right away, almost as soon as she was admitted
to the intensive care unit.

Around two A.M. I tell Mom I'm tired and want to go to
bed. My cot is only a few inches off the floor and is on the
other side of her bed. She won't be able to see me. But, I
assure her, I'll be there all through the night.

"Go ahead," she says, "Go to bed. Get some rest. You
must be exhausted after your long bus trip from California,
you and the boy." She thinks I'm an eighteen-year-old battered wife again. I've left my first husband and have come
home to her with my baby.

"I've been waiting for such a long time. . . . I was just
about to give up on you. If you're hungry . . . I cooked a big
pot of chili." She smiles at me. She knows her chili was my
favorite. "Look on the back burner."

I was going to come home. The last time he beat me, I
decided to leave him for good, once my bruised face healed.
I did leave him and I was going to go home to my mother.
But I changed my mind.

"I've been waiting for you," she says now on her deathbed, lost in time, her mind back in that night long ago when
she waited and waited and I didn't show up.

I was young and all alone with a baby and I had what
amounted to less than ten years of formal education and no
job skills. But what would have become of me had I returned
to Wapato?

I didn't call Mom and tell her I wasn't coming. It became another of her examples of how inconsiderate I was. It was storming the night I was supposed to come home but didn't. She worried I had been in an accident on the road . . . or worse, that my husband had gotten to me before I could get away. She waited and waited all night long, worrying and watching out the windows, expecting the phone to ring.

A long while later she told me that when I first left my husband, he wrote a letter, a very stupid letter, to her. (He was a white man, a college-educated one.) He told her in his letter that I was immature and would rather run away from my problems than face them and work them through. He asked her not to let me come home. She was not helping me, he told her, as she might think by providing me with a place to run away to and hide. She was only encouraging me to continue being immature. He was sure that he and I could "work out our differences" and build a strong marriage if she didn't provide an easy out for me.

Mom said she wrote him a letter "telling him off." She was not a fool, and neither was her daughter. She hadn't raised me to be "anyone's punching bag," she told him, and as long as she was alive, I would have a place I could run away to.

I didn't show up, though she cooked a big pot of chili for my homecoming, though she waited and watched and worried all night long. And I didn't even care enough to pick up the phone and let her know I wasn't coming.

I was absolutely destitute, staying not at a battered-women's shelter but at a welfare hotel. I didn't know a soul in San Francisco except for my husband and his friends. And, yes, I was afraid he would track me down and vent his rage full force on me. And I had a little baby boy. Yet I still felt I was better off staying in San Francisco. I didn't know what I was going to do, but I felt somehow that I had a better chance there. I didn't know how to say it. I didn't want to discuss it. I was worn out and I was afraid. I didn't call my mother, though she was expecting me and all I'd have had to do was pick up the phone.

But now, in her mind, we're in that night in 1965. This time things turn out differently. This time her wait is not in vain. This time, though I am late and she's almost given up on me, I arrive.

Mom is glad I'm home. Glad to see me. Excited. Relieved. She talks about the weather: "Just listen to that wind!" she says. Though that was a stormy night, this night is calm. But she can still hear that wind. How was my trip? she wants to know. What time did I leave San Francisco? (I think that bus trip used to take twenty-two hours.)

I tell her I must go to bed. I'm very tired. I go to my cot on the other side of her and lie down. She's too excited to try to sleep herself. She keeps talking.

I can see her, but she can't see me. My mom, who was so powerful to me. Shrunken, emaciated, her body all bent. How thin her white hair is now. Her life will be over soon. The end is in sight. At last she falls quiet.

I think of her sitting at the kitchen table writing that letter to my ex-husband, telling him off. He must have been surprised to get a letter like that from her.

"Good night, Mom," I call to her.

"Good night, Dear," she answers. *Dear.* She called me *Dear.* She used to call me "Dear" sometimes when I was a little girl. Once in a while when I was older too. I'd forgotten, but now it sounds familiar.

"And listen now, don't you worry about anything," she says. Speaking is very difficult for her now. She is trying hard to use a reassuring tone. Her voice is so weak, her breathing labored. "Don't worry," she tells me. "We'll get by somehow. We always do."

"Okay, Mom. Now you get some rest." We always did get by somehow. Sometimes just barely. I don't know how we got by, but we always did. *Somehow.*

She is surprised to see me the next morning. She is back in the present. She doesn't remember I stayed the night in her room. My middle sister and one of her grown daughters arrive with a hearty breakfast for Mom of scrambled eggs and ham in Styrofoam plates. Of course she won't be able to eat. I leave. I drive around some more. This is so hard.

My sisters are all in town. One at the house and two at hotels, two with their husbands, all with grown children and some with grandchildren. I'm not feeling well. I can't rest here. I can't sleep. I'm not needed here. I've seen my mother. I must leave on a speaking tour soon that will have to support me for the next several months. I decide to go back to Bellingham and try to get some rest before my trip.

I call Wapato before boarding my plane for L.A. International. Mom has slipped into a coma. No chance she'll come out of it. Maybe I shouldn't go ahead with my tour. But if I stay, how will I live? What will I live on? I can't stay. I'm not needed in Wapato. There's nothing I can do there. She is surrounded by her family. She isn't alone. I board my plane.

It takes off and rises higher and higher. At last it reaches a place above the clouds where the sky is a peculiar, pure color of deep blue. I think of heaven and hell and life after death, none of which I believe in. I think of my father waiting for her at the end of the tunnel. His wait is over now.

I am in L.A. when she dies. "At five o'clock sharp," my niece says. "Quitting time."

I call my daughter who is fifteen and lives with her father to tell her her grandmother is dead. My daughter begins to weep. "She was a good old lady," my daughter says. Yes, she was, I say. "She had a hard life," my daughter says. My daughter used to visit Mom every Sunday when she was in the nursing home in Spokane. On Sundays my daughter fed my mother her meals, combed her fine, white hair, read to her. They got to know each other. "I didn't know any old lady could be that smart," my daughter said once. Yes, she *was* smart. And despite the wasting away, the deterioration of her body, the pain she suffered, she never got senile. Only in the last year she began to get confused as to who people were and to lose her place in time. And maybe that was partly due to the drugs she had to take for her various ailments.

"Just think of her as being free," I tell my daughter, who does believe in God. "Now her soul is free. Her suffering is over."

My daughter will attend the funeral. I tell her she will have to represent me and her soldier brother as well as herself. She is the only member of our family who will be able to attend. She says okay.

I call one of my cousins in Spokane and tell him my

mother died. He says he and his sister will take my daughter
with them to Wapato. It's all arranged. My son, who is in the
army, finally calls me back. He's in Louisiana. Swamp com-
bat training (in anticipation of El Salvador?). It seems to me
his speech has something southern about it now. He can't
get leave to attend my mother's funeral.

I make more calls. My youngest sister, the only one who
remained with my mother in the last days, is the one in
charge. They want to put something more than the standard
obituary in the Wapato paper, something really telling something about Mom, something detailed that will cost more.
My sister thinks I might want to write it. I can take part.

In Southern California, near the place where my own life
began, I sit and write my mother's obituary, which is three
times as long as the usual newspaper obituary notice, but is
still very concise. It takes me hours to write it. I tell of her
birth in Canada and that her mother was a Kootenay Indian
and that Mom, through her mother, was descended from
Dr. John McLoughlin, an important figure in Northwest
history (Mom was so proud of being his descendant). I tell
that she was the daughter of an Irish railroad man and had
grown up, therefore, in quite a few places in British Columbia and Washington State. I tell about her husband, my
father, and when they married and when we settled in
Wapato. I say she was crippled by rheumatoid arthritis and
was in a good deal of pain, yet she remained in good spirits
(which she did, for the most part) and her mind remained
clear. I say she will be missed by her large family, which she
will be.

In her last years, I say, she was lovingly attended in her
own home by her granddaughter in Wapato. She is survived

by (I name them) a son, a stepson, and three daughters (in
chronological order, naming myself last), and twenty-three
grandchildren (whom I don't name) and (I leave blank because I don't know how many, my sister will have to fill it in)
great-grandchildren. I don't say three of her children won't
be there: her oldest daughter, who died a few months earlier
of cancer, and her only son, whom she left when he was a
little boy but always cherished anyway, and myself. (She
always told me I wouldn't be welcome at her funeral. "Just
stay away!" That was meant to hurt me, to make me reform
and not cause her any more grief. Did she ever imagine I
might not be there?) I am in Iowa when they bury her.

It's all over by the time I arrive in New Mexico. Oddly this
is the most difficult time. I held up as she lay dying, and
when she died, and in those days before her funeral. But now
that it's all over, I feel like I'm starting to come apart. Maybe
I'm just tired. I don't want to have a relapse. I want to go
home. I am in New Mexico three days, then fly home to
Bellingham.

One week after I get home, I drive to my mother's house.
This will probably be the last time I am ever here. I pay the
mortuary my share of the funeral expenses. My niece, the
one who lived with her and was her caretaker, goes with me
to the cemetery.

The land in the Yakima Valley is flat and, compared to
Idaho, arid. This is a graveyard of strangers enclosed by a
high, chain-link fence. It seems oddly impersonal. Not like
back home in Idaho, where Dad is buried, the place where
all our family graves are. It doesn't seem right that Mom is
here.

My mother's new grave has no marker. My niece has to show me where it is. She, who is not yet twenty-nine, tells me that she will purchase the plot next to Gram's grave for herself. "And over there," she points, "under that little tree. My sister is buried there." My sister had had a baby girl who only lived for three days. That was many years ago. So Mom isn't alone, my niece is saying. The wind is blowing; sand in my eyes, in my hair. Papers and tumbleweeds up against the wire fence.

My mom is gone. In the end there are no resolutions. Only an end.

Epilogue

I inherited a black-and-white photograph of myself as an infant that was taken at our house in Oceanside, California, before we went back home. Mom managed to keep only a few precious belongings through all her years of moving around, running away, going, for one reason or another, from place to place. The photo, which is now forty years old, is one of those.

At home I put it, still in its original cardboard frame that is also forty years old, on the table beside my bed.

I am very little in this picture. I am sitting (but don't look like I can sit up by myself yet) on a bed, a large pillow behind my back propping me up. I am wearing only a diaper. I have shaggy black hair and little almond-shaped black eyes. I look perfectly happy and healthy. I seem to be laughing.

I keep the photograph of myself as a baby on the bedside table where I can look at it whenever I want. I wonder how many times my mother looked at it and thought of me, of us the way we were. After a few days I put it away in a trunk, where I keep my own few precious belongings.

Transitions

The song that always reminds me of the summer I was nineteen is the old Simon and Garfunkel hit, "I Am a Rock." I lived in San Francisco then in a room with a view (and little else), and "I Am a Rock" played several times an hour throughout the day on the Top 40 radio station I listened to.

A young man named Derek, a student who lived in my building, loaned me (and would later give me when my baby son and I moved on) that radio. It was all I had in my room at the top of the stairs, a little furnished attic room in a renovated Victorian on Haight Street near Ashbury. I was virtually penniless, though I got enough welfare to pay the rent and buy enough groceries to keep us going. I had nothing left over for such luxuries as bus fare or to buy a can of soda pop or an ice-cream bar, let alone to pay the price of admission at the movies. My neighborhood was full of people, some young, some not so young, who were dropping out, turning on and tuning in. I didn't have the wherewithal for any of that, though.

Derek loaned me books, whatever was left from his humanities and social sciences courses that couldn't be resold. I read a lot of these books. I had to wash diapers every day by hand and I vomited every time I did. I never did get used to soiled diapers, and my son would not be toilet trained for over a year.

"I am a rock . . . I am an I-I-Island!" played in the
background all that summer.

My son, then a year old, had no playthings. He made do
with cardboard boxes and books and other little odds and
ends. The single mother who lived on the floor below us gave
him some plastic toys for his bath. The weather was always
nice, and we had a park nearby that we went to often. My
son was healthy, strong, beautiful. And, the important thing,
I kept reminding myself, besides having a roof over our
heads and food to eat, was this: We were safe. Safe at last.
I had successfully left my husband, and so far he didn't know
where we were (though I knew that he eventually would.
The welfare office would force him to make child-support
payments to them, and in exchange he would have "visitation rights." But I would cross that bridge when I came to
it. For right then we were safe.).

The last time I'd left him, after a beating, he'd tracked me
down. I don't know how he found me. Maybe someone he
knew had seen me go into the welfare hotel. Maybe he
himself had seen me. Maybe he had seen me one day in the
vicinity and followed me. What he told me, though, he who
was then a psychiatric social worker at San Francisco General Hospital, was that he had guessed that I had gone to
welfare and gotten on Aid to the Indigent (he knew I didn't
have any money) and that I would be using my own (maiden)
name, not his. He had called welfare, he said, identified
himself as a social worker, told the records clerk that I had
been admitted as a patient to San Francisco General and he
needed to know my address and other pertinent information
for his files. She gave him my address over the phone.
Whether or not this was true, I have no way of knowing. But

this was what he told me. He had ways of finding me. At any rate, he did find me and came knocking at my door.

"Who is it?" No answer. Silence. Then more knocking. "Who's there?" Again no answer. I'd been there a week, almost. The only visitors I ever got were the hotel manager's daughters, who were about twelve and thirteen. Who else could it be? Possibly someone from welfare. I opened my door.

He had a big, heavy ashtray from the hotel lobby (though I didn't know what it was at first; I just felt the blow that knocked me to the floor), the kind that isn't meant to go anywhere, with sharp metal handles on each side. This is what he hit me with. The wound near my eye spurted blood like a geyser. It left a scar, an indentation about a quarter of an inch from my right eye.

I also had a bump on one eyelid (I can't remember which one) left over from a black eye inflicted by him. The doctors told me this lump was "an organized blood clot" and could not be removed. They said I would probably have it all of my life. People were always asking me how I got it (salesclerks, people at bus stops, people who interviewed me for jobs). Anyone. Everyone. "How did you get that lump on your eyelid?" they would ask, even though it was only visible when I closed my eyes or glanced down. Or to one side. The lump went away of its own accord about three years after I left the room at the top of the stairs.

I have no fond memories of my first brief marriage to a white man who clearly looked down on me. I was barely eighteen. He was the first person I ever knew, aside from schoolteachers, who had a college education. Was I impressed with that? Maybe I was. Maybe I was impressed because he and his similarly white and college-educated friends marched against U.S. involvement in Vietnam and picketed Bank of America in protest of its discriminatory hiring practices, because they listened to K-Jazz radio and owned expensive stereo equipment to play their jazz and classical records on and they read Jack Kerouac and Henry Miller and Ken Kesey. They were hip. I was not. They rejected the values of their parents' generation. All I knew about was getting by from one day to the next.

Clearly this was not a marriage of equals.

Once he handed me a matchbook cover in front of his hip, jazz-buff friends that advertised "Earn Your High School Diploma at Home by Mail" and said, "This is what you should do!" But had I not dropped out of school I *still* wouldn't have been out of high school yet. I wasn't his age, after all. I was just a kid. But he and his friends got a good laugh out of the matchbook cover "joke."

One day when I was seven or eight months pregnant we went over to Berkeley to see the police haul away the Free Speech demonstrators from Sproul Hall. I had no idea then that this great university would one day be *my* university, that this would be the place that would open a new world to me and lead me back into active involvement in an Indian community. I never thought of a future for myself in those days.

When I had a baby things changed. For his sake, I told myself, I *can* imagine a future. I can be more than I was. I can be strong. I can be a rock.

That was how I came to spend the summer of '66 in a plain, white-walled attic room in the Haight-Ashbury all alone except for my son, and flat broke, making do, waiting for time to pass, for a better day, bored and unspeakably lonely, but safe at last and free, with a lump on one eyelid and a scar by my right eye, listening to Simon and Garfunkel singing about emotional and social isolation.

As the summer wore on, I spent more evenings with Derek, whose room, like himself, was impeccably neat and clean. He was from Jamaica, was a graduate student in physics at San Francisco State College, worked full-time at Bank of America, budgeted every dime. He was one serious, hard-working (and, I thought, uptight) boy. He thought I was aimless, though he didn't say so in as many words.

"Why don't you do something? Go to school? Get a job?"

"I can't, Derek."

"Ain't no such word as *can't.*"

"Hey, Mon," I said, trying to sound sort of like him, "can't you see I've got a little baby and nothing else? I'm all alone. How am I supposed to do something?"

"So . . . you got some plans?"

I didn't, not yet, but if I did, I wouldn't tell him. He told me he came from such wretched poverty, I could not imagine. No American could, he said. When he was a boy, he used to dive for silver coins tourists would toss from ships. But he had become educated. Now he had a future. Once or twice I went out to eat and to a movie with Derek, conscious every minute of the hard-earned money he was spending, uncomfortable because of this and because I knew he thought me lazy. Looking back some years later, I wondered if Derek realized then how young I was or if he imagined I was near his age, which was twenty-three or twenty-four.

A few months later I moved into an apartment in another building in another neighborhood at the end of Castro Street. Derek helped me move, told me to keep the radio and surprised me with a gift of twenty dollars. He told me to call him if I "needed anything." He would drop by once in a while when I lived on Castro Street. I was always glad to see him (and glad to see him leave).

My new apartment was cheaper, larger, better, much better, and there were other young welfare mothers and their babies living in that building, people, in other words, like ourselves. New friends. We welfare girls traded baby-sitting. Sometimes I worked as an office temp and brought home a few dollars. I bought an ancient console television for twenty dollars (I hadn't watched TV in years, since my ex was too intellectual for TV). I got a goldfish. I had girl-friends my own age at last, with babies and no husbands. I wasn't so lonely anymore. I was passably happy then. My little son and I used to dance to the radio (no more "I Am a Rock") to "Wild Thing" and the one that goes "Hot time, summer in the city," and to Bob Dylan singing, "How does it feeeeeeeellll . . . to be on your own . . . like a rollin' stone . . ."

My son used to like to hear about an incident that occur-red when we lived on Castro Street. "Tell me about the time I went out on the edge of the roof of a high building and you got me to come back by tricking me."

He was a fast-moving, rambunctious, full-of-the-devil tod-dler at the time. He liked to run away from me, now that he could run.

We went up on the roof of our building, which was eight

stories tall, one warm, sunshiny day for a little outing. I'd brought a blanket to lie on and a *Cosmopolitan* magazine (which was full of stories about sex and the single girl), the radio Derek had given me, and a few toys for my son. The roof was all safely fenced in with a chain-link fence.

In one corner was a large chicken-wire cage of some sort. Maybe pigeons had been kept there once.

I lay down and began reading my magazine while my son played nearby. Once in a while he would stop playing to dance around a bit if he heard some danceable music playing on our radio. He went inside the cage in the corner. I dozed off a little.

Then suddenly I was wide awake. I sat up and looked around. There was my son standing on the narrow ledge of the roof (about four feet wide) outside the fence. He'd gone through the pigeon cage (if that's what it was) and through a small hole in the wire I hadn't seen.

First I told him to come back in a very stern voice. "You come back here right now!" A wide grin spread across his face. Running-away time. He was about to start running, clumsy little toddler that he was, on that narrow strip of tar and gravel that was all there was between him and eternity.

I dropped to my knees then and held my face in my hands and began to pretend to cry, sobbing loudly. He seemed to give up the idea of running away, at least for the moment, and began to inch back towards the hole in the wire, back towards me and safety. But he seemed to sense a trick and didn't climb through. (As an older child he would remember how I had pretended to cry sometimes to get him to do what I wanted when he was little. I was "shamelessly manipulative," he said. Sometimes I had to be.)

Finally I picked up the paper bag that had contained his toys and my magazine and began pretending to take pieces of candy from it and pop them into my mouth.

"Yum," I said, pretending to chew, "this candy sure is good. Yum, yum."

In no time at all he climbed through the hole in the wire, back into the cage and out of it, and was in my arms, asking for candy.

My ex-husband found us again on Castro Street, but he didn't physically threaten me anymore. I had no phone. No car. No job. No future. I was such a mess, he would say, nothing but a no-class welfare bum. I didn't have a pot to pee in, he would sneer . . . and look at the dump I lived in, what a loser I was. Then I would feel downhearted for a while. My ex had money (not really a lot, but it seemed like a lot to me) drove a nice car, wore good clothes. What did I have? Well, I had my boy. And now that I was rid of my ex, I had myself.

By Christmas I had a boyfriend (a friend of a friend who lived in my building) from England. He was as poor as Derek but was not uptight and hardworking . . . he was a rolling stone (wherever he hung his hat was his home). He was not critical of me. He would play his guitar and sing to me. He would tell me of his travels. Of course he'd been to Paris and Rome. And he had seen the Taj Mahal, too, and the pyramids in Egypt. He was company and, when my ex found out about him, he didn't exercise his visitation rights as often. Then my ex got a better job, which required him to move to a city far from San Francisco. Before he left, he warned me that I had better not ask for more than fifty dollars per month child support when I got the divorce. Fifty dollars was all I asked for.

My boyfriend took me to see *Doctor Zhivago* on my twentieth birthday. Then he was gone. To Australia, I think.

Once, I applied to a program at the Youth Opportunity Center that was for unmarried mothers under the age of twenty-one who were on welfare and didn't have any job skills and were lacking a high school diploma. The federally funded program ran for something like five or six months. Participants were provided money for child care, bus fare, books and supplies, and even a small clothing allowance. Participants would receive training as clerk-typists while earning a high school diploma (in those days I didn't know about the GED, the high school equivalency exam, and I didn't think it was possible for a person to go to college without first finishing high school). I was very excited about the program at the Youth Opportunity Center. I was all set. But on the day I went in to begin my training, I was stopped short by my counselor. She had received my high school transcripts. "You weren't honest with us," she said to me in an angry tone. "You lied to us."

"How did I lie?"

"You said you were sure you could handle our program. Your transcripts are very, very poor. A D in math, a D in English . . . an F in social studies. You hardly even went to school at all. You know as well as I do you don't have what it takes to either become a clerk-typist or to earn a high school diploma." She had already made an appointment for me to interview for a job as a domestic. She handed me the referral card I was to give to my prospective employer. My

interview would be in an hour, "so you'll have to hurry." I
took the referral card from her and, right in front of her face,
I tore it into little pieces and dropped it in the wastebasket.

I had some full-time jobs. One, as a clerk-typist at Southern
Pacific Hospital, I lost because they found out I had lied
about being twenty-four and about having attended college
for two years. Another, at the post office, I had to quit
because of the irregular hours I had to work and problems
finding a reliable sitter.

Then I found out, from a neighbor, that I could go to
open-admissions, tuition-free City College of San Francisco
without having finished high school if I were twenty-one,
which I soon would be. I took the entrance exam at City
College and passed with scores so high I wouldn't have to
take any remedial courses at all but could begin a program
of university-parallel courses that were transferable to any
four-year college or university in California. (My ex, who
was not only white but who lived in one place all of his
growing-up years and always knew he would be going to
college—the man who had so looked down on me—had had
to take a remedial English course when he began college.
Ah, how sweet it was!)

I put my son on a waiting list at a beautiful state-subsi-
dized child-care center. For just seven dollars per week they
would keep him all day, five days a week, and they would
give him a hot breakfast and lunch and late-afternoon snack.

We had to move again—this time to a ratty suite above a
bar between Mission and South Van Ness. (I didn't know my
rights as a tenant in those days . . . and even if I had known
them, I don't think I would have been able to stand up to a

much older, more powerful landlord and assert them. I
tended to let myself get pushed around, as poor people do.)
There were cigarette burns all over the carpet in my new
place. It was the former apartment of a prostitute before she
got busted on drug-related charges. (My new neighbors told
me all about it. It had caused a lot of excitement in the
building. They were all concerned about what had happened to her sweet little poodle after the bust when she was
carted off to jail.) Men were always coming there when I first
moved in, ringing the doorbell at all hours. I would stick my
head out the window and ask them what they wanted and
tell them she was gone. A few of them asked me if I was "a
working girl" too. Not likely.

I bought a bicycle at the Purple Heart Thrift Store and
had a passenger seat put on the back. That was where my
son rode when we went tooling around the city. We would
race down the steep hill at Mission Dolores Park on that bike
and cruise around Golden Gate Park on it. We would go out
to Playland at the Beach and go down the giant wooden
indoor slides. Sometimes we would go to Powell and Market
and ride the cable cars for fun. It only cost fifteen cents for
adults in those days, and children rode free. The most excit-
ing part of the ride would be when a car would slip from its
cable and coast wildly down one of those steep San Francisco hills. We liked that. I heard that doesn't happen anymore.

Shortly before my twenty-first birthday, I was informed by
the day-care center that there would be a space for my son,
provided he was fully toilet trained (he was), in time for the
coming semester at City College. I used one of my old
Wapato girlfriend's Youth Fare Card (for people nineteen

and under) and took the airplane home for a visit. My son's passage was free. It was cheaper flying than it would have been taking the Greyhound bus.

We had a good visit with my parents (they had settled once and for all in Wapato by this time). My mother had just begun to use a wheelchair (this was the first time I saw her in a wheelchair), but she was still able to get herself in and out of bed and into the bathroom. She still liked to cook. She didn't seem to be suffering much anymore . . . or at least she didn't for the few days we were there.

My son and I went with my father to Idaho, to our reservation during that time, about a twelve-hour round-trip by car. He had business to attend to regarding his land and tribal politics, and he was taking me to talk to the tribal chairman, his lifelong friend, regarding an education grant to attend college.

Without some kind of help I didn't know how I could make it. Welfare only gave me $145 per month (my ex sent his $50 child-support payments directly to welfare) and out of that, $95 had to go for rent. After paying the day-care center $7 per week, I would have $28 per month. That $28 would have to cover everything (food stamps in those days were not free. You were required to purchase a certain minimum, I think $25 per month for $100 worth of stamps. I had never been able to purchase this minimum). Food, clothing, and laundry for the two of us and bus fare, books and supplies for myself had to come out of that $28. It just wasn't possible, or so I thought, without some kind of help. My father felt confident that I would get a grant from the tribe.

. . .

I remember our trip to the Coeur d'Alene Reservation as very pleasant, despite the cold, overcast day, and, in Idaho, a light snow. I'd made that same trip with my father or with both parents many times, but this was the first time I'd gone home as an adult. I didn't know it then, but this was the last few days I'd ever spend with Dad, as he would die suddenly, of a heart attack, in March of the following year.

My son had a very good singing voice, even at a very young age (a special gift, I always thought, but he said I just thought so because he was my kid). He began, as we sailed along the highway heading east, to sing like a flute. Dad told him his flute sounded beautiful, and it did. Dad had never heard anything like it. My little boy kept up his flute for a long while, an hour or more. It was a happy flute, but subtle, too, and full of emotional intensity.

This was the first time I thought about connections to people who had come before, connections to the land—about ancestral roots that predated the white society that had superimposed itself onto North America. And this was the first time I thought about my own posterity . . . of the possibility of my own bloodline continuing down through the ages.

I had taken my camera along and I took pictures of what seemed like nothing much when I got them developed and got a look at them: my home, my first home. The wild hills. The tall trees. The snow. I took a picture of Dad too. I insisted. In this photo he's standing under a pine tree, its branches behind his head and the snow is falling lightly. He's still handsome at seventy-five, still looks strong and vital and at least ten years younger than he really is. This was the last picture that would ever be taken of him. I have it still.

.   .   .

We went to the agency and saw the tribal chairman. He assured me that the tribe would send me six hundred dollars as soon as I sent proof of my enrollment at City College.

Two days later, when my son and I were all packed and ready to go to the Yakima airport for our flight back to San Francisco International (my father would drive us—Mom was staying home), my parents, smiling and looking very proud of themselves, presented me with a surprise, two going-to-college presents: a little old Smith Corona type-writer made during World War II but in perfect condition, and one hundred dollars cash. I was overwhelmed. I could tell that they'd planned their surprise together. I knew, too, that for them the purchase of that typewriter and the hundred dollars was a huge outlay. It represented a big sacrifice on their part.

The last time I saw my father, he was standing at the fence at the airport in the snow. We were in the airplane and we could see Dad, but he couldn't see us. My son waved to him and called good-bye. As the small plane began to taxi down the field, Dad waved to us—which made my son think he saw us. I felt like crying, but controlled myself. I didn't want to set a bad (crybaby) example.

Back in San Francisco, my first year of college was most difficult, to say the least. Sometimes non-Indians would say things to me like, "The government pays for your education, doesn't it, since you're an Indian," or "Your tribe helped you out, didn't it?"

My tribe did help me during that first horrible year, but not the way you might think, not in a conventional way. I say "horrible" because some horrible things happened. We had

to move twice, for instance. Once I got the Hong Kong flu
and was so sick, I had to crawl on my hands and knees to get
to the bathroom. But that was during Christmas break, and
somehow we managed, and my boy didn't get the flu. The
worst, or one of the worst, the scariest thing that happened
was my little boy got sick one night, very, very sick. He ran
a high fever and had chills and was delirious. I had no way
of getting him to a hospital. I left him alone in our apartment
and went out to a pay phone about three blocks away and
called the emergency room of the nearest hospital and asked
to speak with a physician. The doctor told me that there was
no time to bring him in; if I didn't act very quickly, he would
soon go into convulsions. He instructed me to give him
aspirin (I had to knock on the doors of ten neighbors before
I got one answer that time of night and borrowed some
aspirin) and to stand him in a tub, ankle-deep, of cool water
and to sponge him all over for about twenty minutes . . . and
then to do it again ten minutes later if he weren't much
better. I only had to do it once. He was much better. By the
next day his temperature was back down to normal and he
was as lively as could be. I had no idea what had caused his
illness.

We had a lot of rough times. The tribe never did send any
money, but they never said they wouldn't, and that was how
they helped. They kept accepting my long-distance calls,
kept telling me my money would be coming soon. "Now it
has to be approved by another committee," or "Now it has
to be sent to Lapwai (the Bureau of Indian Affairs office for
northern Idaho) for final approval," or "Your check will be
issued from the Portland Area Office. This will take a little
time." My money would always be coming soon.

If I had known that all I would have while I went to

college was $145 per month—$28 after rent and child
care—I wouldn't even have attempted it. But that $600
check was always on its way. I can hang on until the first of
the month, I would tell myself. Or, I can do it for just two
more weeks. Not long now. And I would dream of the food
and clothes I was going to buy, and all the textbooks and
pens. Maybe we would take in a movie. Somehow I made it
through my first year. And I passed all of my courses.

Then I spoke with my father's old friend who had assured
me the tribe would be sending me a six-hundred-dollar
education grant that day in Idaho, and he told me he was
really sorry, but they had had no more money at the time I
applied. They approved my application, though, and they
thought maybe they would get some more money during the
school year. They didn't want to tell me there wasn't any
money. They didn't want me to give up hope. I told him I
would never have made it without that hope.

I took the SAT and applied for admission to the University
of California at Berkeley. I was accepted. And I was granted
tuition waivers and scholarships and educational loans. I
would be a welfare mother no more. I was twenty-two years
old.

The
Only
Good Indian

"It has always seemed to me that the heaviest penalty the servants of the Hudson's Bay Company were obliged to pay for the wealth and authority advancement gave them was the wives they were expected to marry and the progeny they should rear. What greater happiness to the father, what greater benefit to mankind than noble children. I never could understand how such men as John McLoughlin and James Douglas could endure the thought of having their name and honors descend to a degenerate posterity. Surely they were of sufficient intelligence to know that by giving their children Indian mothers, their own Scotch, Irish, or English blood would be greatly debased. . . . They were doing all concerned a great wrong. Perish all the Hudson's Bay Company thrice over, I would say, sooner than bring upon my offspring such foul corruption, sooner than bring into being offspring of such a curse."

—H. H. BANCROFT,
The History of Oregon—1884

One of my earliest memories is of being taken to Oregon City to visit McLoughlin House, which was Oregon's first museum.

Oregon City, just south of the metropolis of Portland, Oregon, came before Portland—Portland grew from it. My great-great-grandfather, Dr. John McLoughlin, founded

Oregon City when he built his last house and his lumber mill
there. Today Oregon City blends into Portland. McLoughlin Boulevard connects the two.

McLoughlin House is a magnificent, two-story wood-
frame house, a near-mansion. It looks as though it came
from the East, as though it could have belonged to a New
England sea captain. But it is a Northwest house and it
belonged to the man who, as chief factor for the Hudson's
Bay Company, founded Fort Vancouver (which is just north
of what is today Portland, just across the Columbia River).
Before Fort Vancouver there was nothing here. A valley. A
river. Woods. Wilderness. The small city of Vancouver,
Washington, grew from the fort.

"Don't touch," my mother warned me. "Don't touch a
thing, you hear?" Not even the maroon-velvet-covered ropes
that kept tourists from entering open bedrooms and restrict-
ing them to the narrow strip of red carpet that ran down the
hallways and across the big rooms. "Look. Don't touch!
Don't let go of my hand until we get out of here." Her tone
told me she meant what she said.

The house contained a few things that had belonged to
the McLoughlins: his writing table, a lacquered Chinese
cabinet, a grand piano (for some reason our guide told us the
piano had come via ship from Boston but didn't mention
where the other things had come from), an Oriental rug, a
beautiful long dining table with twelve chairs, each place set
with the McLoughlins' elegant china and silver as if the
family and their guests were about to sit down to dinner. All
the rest of the furniture (like the high-canopied beds with the
little stools people had to step onto to get into bed) hadn't
belonged to the family, but were authentic period pieces. We

were supposed to imagine that this was, more or less, the way
the house had looked when the McLoughlins had lived in it,
that this was the kind of furniture they would have chosen.
My mother told me the people who had built this fine house
for their later years and who lived in it for a long time and
both died here were our relations. We were their descendants. Of course I didn't get it.

Did I understand that Gram, Mom's ma, was my grandmother? And that Gram's husband, who died before I was
born, was my grandfather? Sure. Mom's dad, Sullivan, of
whom Mom was so fond. My grandfather. Sure. I got that.
I knew what grandparents were.

Well, these people, whose house this had been, were
Gram Sullivan's grandparents. Gram's grandpa had been a
very, very important man. Dr. John McLoughlin, who came
from a place called Quebec, was chief factor for the Hudson's Bay Company a long time ago. This was sort of the
same as being governor, my mother said. I didn't know what
a governor was exactly. I was just a preschool child. So I
didn't have an inkling what McLoughlin had been. Actually
he had had more power, as chief factor, than any governor.

In those days the Northwest Territory stretched from
California to Alaska. The Territory was held in joint occupancy by the United States and Great Britain. The Hudson's
Bay Company was the quasi-government, and as chief factor, Dr. McLoughlin was its head. His word was law in the
Northwest Territory. It was his domain. He was called King
of the Columbia and Emperor of the Northwest (and posthu-
mously, officially, the Father of Oregon). He became chief
factor in 1821 and ruled for a twenty-one-year period that
came to be known as "The Age of McLoughlin." That

important man was my gram's grandpa, and his wife, Margaret (my mother's name too), was from a place called Ontario, and she was my gram's gram.

I held my mother's hand and looked up at their portraits, not understanding what these people were to me.

Dr. John McLoughlin (Mom and Gram insisted on the proper, Canadian, pronunciation: "McGLOCKlin," rather than the American "McLAWFlin") certainly looked formidable in his portrait, painted when he was in middle age. He was a powerfully built man (he stood six feet four inches tall—a giant of a man in his day—which was 1784–1854) with a stern countenance and dressed in a formal black suit. His hair, a long, wild white mane, flowed well past his shoulders. He was famous for his hair. I would learn much later that it was said to have turned white overnight when his canoe overturned on Lake Michigan during the Great Fur War, when he was in his twenties. The Indians of the Territory called him "The White-Headed Eagle."

Margaret McLoughlin is an old woman in her portrait, which is a photograph, not a painting. She is also wearing black. Maybe because she was a widow then. Maybe old women in her day always wore black. Her hair, though she is in her seventies, is still mostly dark. She wears it parted in the middle and neatly pinned back. Mrs. McLoughlin is dressed like a white woman. *But she is not white. She is an Indian.*

She was a Chippewa, my mother told me. "Doctor McLoughlin was not ashamed of her," my mother said, as though it were mighty big of him not to have been.

Not ashamed of her? I studied her portrait. Solemn. Sad eyes. An Indian woman. What was there about her to be ashamed of? (My mother said things like that sometimes. I didn't like it.) I resented my great-great-grandfather then, the eminent Dr. John McLoughlin, disliked him even. How dare he have such a condescending attitude towards his own wife? I resented Dr. McLoughlin as if my mother's attitudes were his.

There is another memory that goes with the one of our visit to Oregon City:

"White people respect good Indians," my mother said rather casually as she sat darning socks and mending small tears in our clothes. I was about four at the time. I sat on the floor beside her chair, coloring in my (probably Carmen Miranda) coloring book. "Good Indians are clean and neat, hardworking and sober," she said. I wanted to get away from her. I hated it when she talked like that and I could not, even to myself, articulate my feelings because I was too young. I couldn't get away because it was raining. She wouldn't let me out. No escape. "White people look down on the other kind, the bad ones, the drunken, lazy louts." I stopped coloring and went to a window and watched the rain pour. Mom's voice droned on.

She would often instruct me on being a good Indian, the kind white people approve of (and sometimes, when I was a little older, on being the kind of woman men respect). I would feel the resentment rise in my blood. Why should I care? Why don't they worry about being the sort of person I respect? Why should I have to be the one to live up to someone else's expectations? Anyway trying to be a "good Indian" was a futile endeavor. Several years before Gram Sullivan was born, General Sheridan had made his famous remark regarding the only good Indian being a dead Indian. I didn't care to be a good Indian.

. . .

Gram Sullivan was born Angeline McLoughlin (in Idaho or British Columbia) in the Kootenay Valley near the international boundary in 1875. Her father (or her pa, as she called him) was the only surviving son of Dr. John and Margaret McLoughlin. David McLoughlin, Gram's pa, had gone to university and medical school in Paris, France (where his father's brother was then personal physician to the king of France). And of course his father was the wealthiest, most powerful man in the whole Northwest Territory. Yet, Gram's pa did what many half-breed Indian boys before him had done: he just saddled up his horse and rode away. He left the white world behind and wandered for a time before he came to the beautiful Kootenay Valley. He married a full-blooded Kootenay Indian woman named Annie Grizzly, who became Gram's ma.

Gram Sullivan was actually one-quarter white (that one quarter coming from her paternal grandfather, Dr. McLoughlin), but Gram was a *dark* Indian woman, much darker than I. As dark as my other grandmother, who was a full-blood. She was part white, but she had the looks of a full-blood.

She was paralyzed on her left side and lost the power of speech when she suffered a stroke when I was about six. I have no memories of her before the stroke. To me she was always a mean-looking old woman sitting in a wheelchair, one arm in a sling. She couldn't speak, but she made ugly, scolding noises that sounded like swearing. She "swore" at everyone. She had a reputation for being mean. Before the stroke she was mean, and after, she was meaner still. She also had a reputation for not liking us, the children of my mother's second marriage. (She remained on friendly terms with my mother's ex-husband, who was white, and saw the children—a boy and a girl—from this marriage regularly.)

I do have one memory, not of her exactly but of a conversation, a short exchange between my mother and me before Gram's stroke:

We're at Gram's house in Spokane, in the bathroom. I'm upset. My mother is upset too. Maybe I've been crying because Mom's washing my face with cold water. "Why does Gram hate me?" I ask.

"She doesn't hate you. Don't think that. She hardly even knows you. She's just old and cranky. And . . . you remind her of someone else . . . someone she does hate." The words sink in, and I remember them always. *I remind her of someone she hates.* Who?

I thought my father must be the one I reminded Gram of, because she did hate him. That was no secret. My mother alone, of seven Sullivan children, married an Indian, went to live on a reservation, and had Indian kids. My mother's sisters all looked one hundred percent white, just like Mom. They were poor, uneducated, working-class, yet made no effort to disguise the fact they looked down on us because we were Indian.

Clearly there was no love lost between my father and my mother's family. Surely he must be, I thought, the one I remind Gram of. People said I looked like him.

Though Dad never spoke a word against Gram or indicated in any way that he disliked her, he wasn't overly subtle when it came to what he thought of my mother's sisters: "So, you're going with your mamma to visit her sisters today? Good. I want you to do something, okay?" I nodded. Sure.

Anything. "I want you to watch your aunts and listen to them. Observe them very carefully. You know why? Because the way those women are . . . that's just exactly the way women should not be." I could learn a lot from them, Dad said. Watch their every move. But don't let them catch me watching them. I took him seriously and did as I was told. I furtively observed my aunts.

They were loud and aggressive and argumentative. My mother spoke softly (most of the time). They did not. They were rude and crude. They smoked and drank. They swore and said "shit" a lot. They made stupid, snide remarks about Indians, too, whenever they could. For instance, there was the time one of my aunts had seen a man looking into a neighbor's window. She went out in the dark night and fired her little handgun (which she kept for her "personal protection") into the sky and scared the Peeping Tom away. Though it was very dark, my aunt said she could tell the peeper was an Indian because he had an Indian shuffle. He fled into the night with an Indian shuffle, she said. Mom just ignored this reference, as she ignored all of their references and snide remarks. Then, most of the time, she fumed over them when we got home. She just laughed about the guy with the Indian shuffle, though, imagining him running and shuffling at the same time in a way that was so distinctive, her sister could tell, even in the dark, that he was an Indian.

So my aunts smoked, drank, swore and were vulgar, not to mention racist. But they were kind to their mother. They took care of her for many, many years. They put up with her nagging (the noises she made to express her unhappiness) without complaint. Gram was known to knock her food away with her good arm, causing it to fly across the room. Once they brought her an alphabet, large plastic letters.

Since she didn't seem interested in writing when they brought her a pencil and paper, they thought maybe she would communicate with them by putting these plastic letters together to form words. They put the letters in front of her on a low table and explained to her what they had in mind. Gram got very, very angry and began yelling at them, making those awful noises of hers and then knocked the table over. She didn't want to form words, they thought. It was too tedious for her. (Much later, when I was grown, I remembered the incident and thought Gram had probably lost the ability to read or write, as stroke victims do. She probably couldn't form words with plastic letters any more than she could write with a pen. But that didn't occur to my aunts.) Gram was mean and cranky and hard to put up with. She had, in fact, always had a bad disposition. But they took care of her and were patient with her, too, and as kind as they could be.

They said she'd worked so hard when they were children. She had made so many sacrifices for them. "Now it's our turn," they'd say. "Now we must take care of her."

Their father, who had worked for Great Northern Railroad, had had some sort of work-related accident one winter day. He was pinned under something. It took a long time to free him. He'd been exposed to the cold for a long period of time. The result was frostbite. His toes had to be amputated, and he was out of commission for a long while.

That was long before President Roosevelt's New Deal. No workmen's compensation then. No state disability. No unemployment benefits. No Aid to Families with Dependent Children. Nothing. And six children to feed.

Gram Sullivan took in laundry (there were a lot of single

men in the railroad camps). Railroad men's clothes must
have gotten very dirty. Of course she had no running water,
no washing machine.

Gram worked hard as a laundress, harder than seemed
humanly possible. Gathering laundry, chopping wood,
building fires, hauling water, heating tubs of it and scrubbing, scrubbing the clothes on a washboard. Her hands got
all raw. The skin on her knuckles cracked and bled. But she
managed. Gram did it. She supported her family of eight for
one whole winter and spring all on her own. "And now it's
our turn," her daughters who weren't refined said when she
got old, crippled, speechless and crabby. And they did take
care of Gram. They took good care of her.

Spokane, even today, is a sort of wild-West kind of town.
Country western music is, and has always been, very big in
this region and lots of men wear cowboy boots and drive
pickup trucks with gun racks. And it's conservative. Very
conservative. It's surrounded by five Indian reservations (including my own, which is about sixty or seventy miles east
of the city. The first Kootenay rez is about one hundred
miles north.). If you are an Indian in Spokane, you are
always aware of it. There is not a great multitude of people
from many diverse ethnic and racial backgrounds. (I don't
recall ever seeing a black person in Spokane until I saw one
walking down the street one day when I was thirty years old.)
In Spokane no one ever mistakes me for Hispanic or Middle
Eastern. No one there has ever asked me, as I've often been
asked in New York and San Francisco, "What is your ethnic
background?" They know what it is.

Even today, in Spokane, Indians pretty much keep to
themselves and whites to themselves, though there are peo-

ple on both sides striving for racial harmony. But there's a word that was used to describe an Indian, a "dirty," denigrating word, sort of like *nigger*. The word is *Siwash*. My parents first told me about that word and told me I should just ignore it if I heard it, that I should feel sorry for a person who would say it because such a person has a bad heart and is ignorant.

It was sort of like *squaw*, but worse. *Siwash*. It had the power to cut like a knife. "Dirty Siwash." The last time I heard it was on the street in Spokane when I was thirty-one. A group of young white men in cowboy boots who had obviously been drinking passed me. One of them turned his head and looked back (but didn't slow his pace) and muttered, "Siwash. Goddamned Siwash." I was startled. I'd even forgotten such a word existed. It still had the power, after all those years, to cut like a knife.

That was what my mother's first husband called her, she told me when I was older. Despite her beauty. Despite her white looks. Nobody could tell she wasn't white if they didn't know. Her husband knew. And he was one of those people my parents told me about. "Squaw," my mother's first husband would call her when he felt mean, which was a lot of the time. "Stupid Siwash squaw. That's all you are, you know. Just a Siwash squaw." The psychological wound he suffered when she left him for a full-blood must have been deep.

So Mom had had to suffer racial slurs, too, as I had when I was growing up. Probably not just at the hands of her first husband either. She and her white-looking sisters, after all, couldn't hide their mother very easily (nor, I think, did they wish to hide or deny her).

I didn't know Gram Sullivan before her hair turned white

and don't remember her before she was an invalid and her daughters began to keep her hair cut short and neat and easy to care for. My mother and aunts said Gram's hair had been thick, blue-black and smooth as satin. She often wore it, when she wasn't working (and it had to be pinned up), hanging loose. It fell nearly to her waist.

Gram Sullivan's hair was like black satin. The looks of a full-blood. But not the soul of one. Not like Poulee, my other grandmother, who spoke not a word of English, never wore a pair of shoes in her life and was nothing if not secure in her idea of herself, her acceptance of herself as an Indian woman. Not a Siwash. Not a squaw. An Indian woman.

My mother identified very strongly with her Irishness. Maybe because she looked Irish. Maybe because she was her Irish grandparents' favorite person in all the world. Her happiest childhood memories were of staying with them on their farm. Mom knew all about County Clare, where they had come from, and she could speak with an Irish brogue just like theirs. She did speak with an Irish brogue, a little, every Saint Patrick's Day.

Mom enjoyed the social life of the railroad camps too. Feast days. Parties. Dances. Even a wake was a social event. Once, Mom won a local beauty contest. I don't know what the title was, but it was a little like homecoming queen in that the railroad men all voted for the girl they believed the fairest one of all. It was a highly coveted honor. Mom didn't expect to be chosen—partly because she didn't believe she was beautiful, ever, no matter what anyone said, and because she was years younger than the girls, of marriageable age, who did expect to be chosen.

They were all gathered at this yearly event, a party and

dance that children as well as adults attended. The time came to announce the homecoming queen (or whatever she was called). They called out the name: "Maggie Sullivan." That was Mom! The older girls, the girls who would be queen, were shocked. One of them wept. But Maggie Sullivan was happy and she would never forget that time, not ever.

Gram Sullivan was the only nonwhite wife in that society. She didn't participate in any of it, Mom said. She had no friends. When her husband and children went to the wakes and parties and dances and feasts, Gram stayed home alone. She had things to do, she would say, you all go ahead and have a good time. Or she would have a headache. Or she would want to relax and enjoy a little peace and quiet. Mom said she thought Gram felt inferior because she wasn't Irish. I wonder if this was true. Did the woman who washed so much dirty Irish laundry that year her husband was disabled feel inferior because she wasn't Irish?

Gram loved her home in the Kootenay Valley and went back for visits. She didn't take her children with her, though, unless they were babies. Sometimes Gram's Kootenay relatives came to visit her. They could not (or would not) speak English. Gram and her relatives always conversed in Kootenay when they came to visit. She always dressed in whitewomen's styles, but her relatives did not.

Mom remembered herself as a little girl hiding behind her mother's skirts and peeking at the Kootenay visitors. They wore moccasins and leggings and bright-colored clothing, and their hair (even the men's) was in long braids. They did not wear coats. They wrapped themselves in blankets (I imagine wool trade blankets from the Hudson's Bay Company) and wore exotic jewelry made of shells and animal's teeth and glass beads. Some of them wore earrings my mother especially admired that were large and made of some sort of shells. Mom coveted those earrings and imagined herself, when she was grown, wearing them. (Only, Mom would be much too conservative to wear any sort of flashy jewelry, let alone Indian shell earrings.)

Mom was afraid of her mother's exotic relatives, but she was attracted to them, too, fascinated by them. She liked the way they looked. She loved to listen to the smooth, flowing language she didn't understand. She knew Gram's Kootenay grandpa had been a chief, and she liked to imagine him and what he must have been like. For all her Irishness, I think Mom always felt a strong Indian undercurrent in herself.

My grandfather Sullivan was the youngest child of a large family. He was born in County Clare, Ireland, in about 1871. When he was just an infant his father slaughtered and butchered his own hog without paying the tax required by law. He was caught in the act by a British tax collector, who then tried to impose not only the tax but also a fine for attempting to evade the tax.

Times were bad in Ireland. The government did things to the Irish people—forbade them to speak Gaelic, collected all their potatoes and sold them back to them, imposed all sorts of taxes on them.

So, the story goes, my grandfather's father was caught in the act. Still holding the knife he had used to butcher the hog, its blood still warm on the sharp steel blade, he killed the tax collector. He then went underground and, with the help of his friends in the resistance, got out of Ireland. His wife and children escaped by pretending to be the wife and children of his half brother, whose name was not Sullivan. Friends and neighbors gave my mother's grandmother a gold broach the night before they left. It had a pair of manacled hands engraved on it symbolizing the oppression of the Irish people by the British government.

My grandfather must have been two or three when his mother snuck out of Ireland, snuck them all out, with the help of her brother-in-law. He and his family were part of those famous huddled masses yearning to breathe free. But he had no memory of the country he came from (no feeling for it, either, as his parents had. No nostalgia. No desire to return to it). He had no memory of the voyage, of arriving in America.

The Sullivans settled in New York City, which was not hospitable to Irish immigrants at the time. Employers advertised for help but noted NO IRISH NEED APPLY and some businesses put signs in their windows that said, NO DOGS OR IRISH ALLOWED. My grandfather's parents never did like New York. Their older children soon reached adulthood and married and had children of their own. It looked like they would be stuck in that big, mean city for good.

Then, when the man who killed the British tax collector and his wife were past middle age, homesteading opened up in Idaho and Washington State. Good, rich farmland, free for the taking (which, of course, was available because the American government had taken it from the Indians of the

West). Despite their age, and the fact that they had just one
child at home (the almost-grown young man who would
become my mother's father), the Sullivans went west and
again had at long last a farm of their own! My mother never
knew any of the cousins, aunts or uncles Sullivan who remained in New York City.

My grandfather went to work for Great Northern when he
grew up. Somewhere along the line, as he was laying tracks
(no doubt in Kootenay country), he met an Indian girl
named Angeline.

She must have seemed a strange Indian girl, not at all
"shy" as Indian girls were always said to be. And she spoke
English. Not just fluently but really well, like an educated
person. And she could read and write too. A most unusual
Indian maiden.

Angeline McLoughlin became Mrs. Sullivan and left the
Kootenay Valley.

I was fourteen when Gram Sullivan died. She was eighty-
five. I remembered that day at her house before she had her
stroke when she made me cry and my mother told me I
wasn't to think she hated me. "She's just old and cranky,
that's all. And . . . you remind her of someone else . . .
someone she does hate."

None of my sisters attended Gram's funeral, though most
of her grandchildren and great-grandchildren did. We buried her in Spokane beside her husband. Then my parents
and I went home to Wapato, and I didn't think of that
crabby old woman for years and years.

Then suddenly, after a long time had passed, I began to

think of her. I remembered her face and the photographs I'd
seen of her when she was young and the stories my mother
and aunts told about her. What had Gram really been like?
Who, if anyone, had I reminded her of?

I read a book about Gram's tribe. The Kootenay was the
only tribe in the region that had been matrilineal, the only
one that had had women warriors.

I remembered a book my mother had owned, a biography
of Gram's granddad, Dr. John McLoughlin, and his brother
and sister, entitled *The McLoughlin Empire and Its Rulers*. It was
a big, heavy, formidable-looking book. Royal-blue cloth with
gold lettering. It looked important. It had been very important to Mom. To her it said she came from "a good family,"
whatever her (our) circumstances might be. From a good
family . . . but down on her luck. She read it often, studied
it. *Interpreted* her ancestors.

I was never interested in that book. I didn't like my
mother's interpretations of the McLoughlin family. Their
lives, I thought, had no relevance to my own. Who was Dr.
John McLoughlin, after all, but a big, rich white man who
had exploited Indians in the old days? Father of Oregon.
What did that mean? Helped settlers steal land. I wasn't
impressed.

Of course I had to study Northwest history in school, and
every Northwest-history textbook told about Dr. John
McLoughlin. Once, just once, I raised my hand in class and
told my teacher, "He was my great-great-grandfather." I
must have been about eight years old at the time. My teacher
didn't say a word, just stared at me, stared hard. Some of my
classmates giggled. When I told my mother, she said I should

never mention that I was related to Dr. McLoughlin. Nobody would believe me. I would be ridiculed. I never did
mention it again. So why would I be interested in his life?
Why would I want any part of him?

But now, years later, for some reason I *was* interested. Dr.
John McLoughlin's life was relevant to Gram's life. And
Gram's life was, somehow, relevant to my own.

I got myself a copy of *The McLoughlin Empire and Its Rulers.*
It was still a formidable-looking book. We were all there on
a family chart: Gram's ma and pa and all Gram's children,
including Mom (and even Dad's name was there, as Mom's
husband), my sisters . . . and *me.*

In 1983 I applied for a sixty-day residency fellowship to go
to the Center for the Study of the History of the American
Indian at the Newberry Library in Chicago. I wanted to
study the fur-trade era in North America, the white-Indian
marriages of that time, and the mixed-blood people, who
were (and are) a legacy of the fur trade.

I wanted to study the McLoughlin family, to study Old
Fort Vancouver so long and so hard Fort Vancouver in its
heyday would take form in my imagination.

Fort Vancouver was many things of course. Headquarters
for the Hudson's Bay Company (that is, of the fur trade) in
the Northwest Territory. It was a thriving cultural center,
too, known as the Paris of the West. It was also a fully
functioning military fort, not out of fear of the many Indian
tribes that lived in the Territory, who were the business
partners of the Hudson's Bay Company, but because American aggression was feared. Fort Langley, just south of what

is today Vancouver, British Columbia (and a long way north of Vancouver, Washington), was the second fort McLoughlin built in the West, intended as a backup in case Americans attacked Fort Vancouver, and put it out of commission.

The dispute over the boundary was a serious one. A war was nearly fought over it. Great Britain wanted the Columbia River to be the dividing line. This was why McLoughlin built Fort Vancouver on the north bank of the river. This was where Canada was to begin (where the state of Washington actually begins). Americans were not in agreement. In 1844 James Polk's campaign slogan was "54.40 or Fight," referring to where he wanted the border to be (that is, at the southern tip of Russian Alaska). Chief Factor McLoughlin built Fort Vancouver when Gram's pa was just a little boy. Her pa had grown up there. Before prep school in Montreal. Before university in Paris. Before he went Native.

I wanted to imagine, if I could, Gram's early life before she left the People of the Valley and married Sullivan and became my mother's ma. What made her the way she was when I knew her? What had she been like before?

I was awarded the research fellowship and went to Chicago the summer of 1984.

Gram Sullivan's paternal grandfather, Chief Factor Dr. John McLoughlin, was born in 1784 in Rivière-du-Loup (River of the Wolf), Quebec. (*His* grandfather, Captain Malcolm Fraser, came from Inverness, Scotland, to fight for the British on the Plains of Abraham. He was my first non-

Indian ancestor in North America. Years later, now a colonel, Malcolm Fraser fought for George II against the Americans during the revolutionary war. He defeated
Montgomery (who was killed in battle) and the soon-to-be-
infamous General Benedict Arnold at the Battle of Quebec
on the last day of 1775. As a reward for saving Quebec—it
had been a close battle, and Montreal had already fallen—
His Majesty rewarded Colonel Fraser with the seigneury at
Mount Murray, Quebec. But all of that is another story. His
grandson joined the fur trade. He only meant to stay in the
business for a brief while. But he met a woman named
Margaret at his first post, a Chippewa Indian woman.

Margaret was no nubile Indian maiden. She was ten years
his senior and the mother of four young children. She had
been abandoned, as most Indian women involved in liaisons
with white men of the fur trade eventually were, by her first
white "husband."

Dr. John McLoughlin knew very well that he could not
hope to return to Montreal and the genteel life he had
imagined for himself with an Indian wife (not to mention
four half-Indian stepchildren). John and Margaret married,
and from then on his life was the fur trade. It had to be.
Eventually he was appointed chief factor and went to the
Northwest Territory, where he founded Fort Vancouver.

Gram's maternal grandfather was also born in the 1780s, but
the exact date, the exact year, is unknown. (Like her other
grandfather, he died before Gram was born.)

Gram's maternal grandfather was a Kootenay (which
is an anglicized version of the tribe's name for itself:
"Kul:nee," which means "People of the Valley.") He had

been kidnapped, taken as spoils of war, by the Blood Indians, who were the bitter enemy of the Kootenay, when he was just a little boy. They kept him as their slave and were unimaginably cruel to him. His was a wretched existence growing up among the Bloods. At age fourteen he escaped and returned home to the People of the Valley.

Shortly thereafter a Grizzly Bear appeared to him in a vision and told him he was destined to become a great war chief and Grizzly himself, the fiercest, strongest, bravest one of all, would be his animal protector, would counsel him and ride into battle with him. That was how Gram's grandfather became Chief Grizzly—one fierce war chief—the most effective killer of Blood Indians that ever lived.

It appears as though Chief Grizzly converted to Catholicism in his later years. His children took Christian names (though he did not. Maybe only his children and their mother converted.), and the English translation of his name, that is, of his animal protector, became their surname.

Annie Grizzly, Gram's ma, never learned English. Annie died when Gram was still a young girl, and Gram, the bossiest and eldest, took over the housekeeping and looked after the others. Her pa, who lived to be a very old man, never remarried.

Since they lived in a remote area where no school existed, I presume it was their pa (it had to be) who taught Gram and her sisters to speak English so well and to read and write.

When Gram's pa, David McLoughlin, left his wealthy, mixed-blood family and went Native, there most certainly was a great deal of racial prejudice against Indians and those of mixed blood. There had always been, but it became more intense as the fur-trade era began to fade and the missionaries came, followed by floods of white settlers with their insatiable hunger for land.

I think David became disgusted with politics (he left Fort Vancouver shortly after his only brother was assassinated as part of a plot to oust his father from power). David had been, until then, a dutiful son . . . but he truly had no desire for power as his father had had, no desire to head a dynasty. David preferred the wilderness and the Native way of life. (I've read his letters. In one, to his best friend and cousin, David Michaud, with whom he'd studied in Paris, he wrote that the years in Europe seemed only a dream now that he was home on the frontier.)

"There's something wrong with every one of them," HBC governor Sir George Simpson said of mixed-bloods, he who had many Indian children by many different Indian women, most of whom he did not acknowledge and did nothing for. (Some of the Frasers had urged Dr. McLoughlin not to marry his Indian wife . . . and then not to educate his children: "A good education is wasted on a boy with Native blood.") David had grown up with anti-Indianism, though his father's wealth and authority and his own light skin had protected him to a degree. But he could hardly foresee the racism of the society that would replace the one he'd known, the society that would regard Indians as subhuman beings, as soulless savages to be done away with so that the West could be won.

He was just a half-breed who preferred the Indian way of life when he went to the wilderness and married a woman named Annie Grizzly and lived out his long life as an Indian. He could not imagine the sort of life the next generation of Indians, including his own children, would have.

. . .

When Gram was a year old, in 1876, General Custer led the 7th Cavalry to the Battle of Little Big Horn, which not one white man survived. Sitting Bull fled to Canada, where he was granted political asylum. Never were Indians more unpopular in the United States of America than in 1876 after Custer's Last Stand.

In 1879, when Gram was four years old, Carlisle Indian School, in Pennsylvania, opened its doors for the first time. Carlisle was the first government-run boarding school, the first attempt to assimilate Indians, en masse, into mainstream society.

They rounded up students-to-be, not extremely young children but older ones and adolescents, from reservations all over the United States and brought them by freight train to Pennsylvania. Many died of disease and homesickness. A few committed suicide rather than become "a white man's Indian."

Many people thought the best solution to what was commonly referred to as the Indian Problem, (that is, what to do with the Indians who had survived the Indian wars, the ones living on reservations) was to kill them all off. To just exterminate them as though they were cockroaches.

The director of Carlisle, though, was humane and progressive. His motto was: "Kill the Indian and Save the Man." Get rid of everything Indian . . . his language and culture, his identity. Cut his long hair short. Make him wear white people's clothes. Then he would be all right.

Carlisle (whose most famous graduate was the great athlete Jim Thorpe) was considered a success. The government established more Indian schools, patterning them after Carlisle, in Oklahoma, Arizona, Nebraska, South Dakota, Utah, New Mexico, Kansas, California, and Oregon. It supported many other, church-operated residential schools. Whether run directly by the government or by a church through a government contract, all the Indian schools had the same goal: assimilation. The residential schools were notorious hellholes.

When men from the government came to Kootenay country, the Kootenay hid their children, but many were found and taken away. Gram and her sisters, though, were spared. There was no reason to haul them away to government school. They spoke English as well as, or better than, any white children around. And they could read and write like nobody's business. They were allowed to stay home.

When Gram was fifteen years old, in 1890, the slaughter at Wounded Knee occurred. Surely she was aware of it. It was big news. She read newspapers. She probably read anything she could get her hands on.

What did she think when she read about all those Indians in South Dakota who had been shot down like dogs because they, unarmed and all penned in, had been singing Indian songs, Ghost Dance songs, that made the white soldiers who guarded them nervous? (Did the newspapers of the day, I wonder, publish those photographs taken at Wounded Knee of the frozen corpses lying in the snow? Did the accounts in the papers tell how the soldiers took articles of clothing and even cut body parts from the corpses to take away as souvenirs of Wounded Knee? Did the newspapers print the photograph of the long trench the soldiers dug, of the Indian bodies all piled into it, the mass grave?)

What did Gram think about when she read, or heard,

about the massacre at Wounded Knee and all the rest? When she read about the government's intentions to educate the Indian out of the Indian . . . when she read about her own people described as savages?

All the Indian nations were conquered now, restricted to reservations, forbidden to hunt buffalo, to practice their traditional religions. This was perhaps the darkest hour of the Indian people. The old way was gone, or at least deteri- orating, breaking apart. The People of the Valley became poorer as time passed and their way of life, their traditional way, could not continue (not the way it had been in the days of Chief Grizzly).

Gram was aware of a world beyond the Kootenay Valley. I wonder if she ever daydreamed of the life her father had had before (which he would not discuss with his family) . . . did she daydream of seeing the places he'd seen: Paris, maybe . . . London? Did Gram ever wish she could go back to Oregon from whence her pa had come and reclaim some- thing, at least, of what rightfully should have been hers? I have reason to think she did.

Chicago in the summer is hot, awfully hot for a person from the Northwest, and muggy. But not in the vaults of the Newberry Library, where precious old documents and books are kept. In there I had to wear a sweater to keep warm. My hands got cold.

The Oregon State Historical Society and the Oregon Pioneer Association invited Gram's pa to Portland in 1901 for "Pioneer Day," to be present at a ceremony honoring his father.

More than forty years had passed since David McLough-

lin left white society. Much was made about how the old
man wore Indian buckskins and didn't even own a suit of
white man's clothes. George H. Himes, who held various
offices in both the Historical Society and the Pioneer Association, wrote the old man a letter informing him that a suit
and a pair of shoes had been purchased for him and would
be sent along with a postal money order in the amount of $16
to pay for his train ticket and other expenses. Himes went on
to say that he did not want David to feel that "this is a matter
of charity," for poverty is no crime. "Whatever is done for
you is done for the sake of honoring your father." Himes
advised David to buy a round-trip ticket since he could "save
a little" that way.

A Mr. Ryan wrote a letter to Mr. Himes telling him, "By
request of friends of David McLoughlin I accompanied him
to Spokane and took charge of the $16 you sent. Of this I
expended for him the following sums:

> Round-trip fare from Spokane to Portland, $5.10 (he
> probably had to travel by horse from his home to
> Spokane, a distance of some one hundred and twenty
> miles) and three meals, $1.05.   TOTAL: $6.15

Bed at the Pacific Hotel, $.75; shirt, $1.00; underclothes, $1.00	$2.75
Necktie, $.25; handkerchief, $.75	$1.00
Telegram, $.55	$ .55
Lunch to take on the train, $.50	$ .50
GRAND TOTAL	$10.95

"The balance of $5.05 I will give him with his ticket after
I put him on the train to Portland. The old gentleman has

lived in the woods so long that he is helpless as a child in a city."

Mr. Himes said about Gram's pa, "David McLoughlin was a very well-educated man, but throwing himself away as he did, destroyed his future. In some respects the visit to Portland in June was not a kindly act. The motive was to, through him, pay tribute to his father. It was a revelation to David of his wasted life."

Reading that made me angry. I wished I'd been there. I would have told the old man not to go. Those people don't really wish to honor your father, I would have said him. They don't have any understanding of who Dr. John McLoughlin was.

They believed David had "thrown himself away" because he'd chosen to live as an Indian. "Don't go, Great-grandpa," I would have said had I been there. "Don't do it. They're going to bring you all that way and dress you up in some stupid white man's suit and make a big deal out of the few cents they paid for it. Many years later a professor of Northwest history who is also a Historical Society member will write a book in which she interviews an old man who was a nine-year-old boy in 1901 and saw you at the Pioneer Day celebration and she will quote him as saying you were 'not well dressed at all' *in your cheap new white-man's suit* 'but rather unkempt and seedy-looking.' And they're all going to shake their heads over your life, which they will regard as wasted, and they'll pity you and write about how you married a *squaw* (as though this were evidence of a wasted life, an illustration of how low you had sunk)."

(They'll even tell *me*, when I visit the replica of Old Fort Vancouver in 1987, how Dr. John McLoughlin had had to marry a squaw because no white women were available on the frontier. A guide will tell me that, not realizing that Dr. John McLoughlin lived on the frontier partly because he had an Indian wife, not the other way around.) "Don't go," I would have said to Gram's pa if I could. "You were right to have left those people when you did. Don't go back. Not even for one day."

But I wasn't there, and he did go. Curator Himes and others wrote letters back and forth on the advisability of bringing a member of David's family to Portland to accompany him, since David was an old man and couldn't walk without the aid of a cane.

In the end they decided against it because, as they put it, no member of his family was "presentable" enough to come to the ceremony they were planning to honor David's father. *Presentable?* Who wasn't presentable? What were they talking about? Their clothing? Then it dawned on me: *presentable* was their euphemism for "white-looking." So. None of his family were light enough. David himself was rather light. His looks were acceptable to Oregon's Historical Society. But no member of his family was. Not Gram. They didn't want her there, nor any of her sisters. (They certainly wouldn't have wanted his mother there either, were she alive. She was too dark for them too). Gram's pa, as old and feeble and forgetful as he was, made that long, trip alone. And they believed they were honoring his father!

I also found, to my great surprise, an account by a woman who was a member of the Society concerning two young Indian women who had come to Portland a few years earlier:

They presented themselves as granddaughters of Dr. John McLoughlin and asked for assistance in seeking employment "and escape from their unenviable surroundings." They seemed to think they were deserving of some sort of special consideration because of who their grandfather had been. Because of their lack of education and unpresentable appearance, they were not suited for any sort of employment save that of washer women. Unsuccessful in their efforts to find work, they left Portland and returned to their home.

My gram! It had to be. Gram at the age of nineteen and one of her sisters! What a great distance they had traveled from their home on the Idaho-Canada border to Portland, Oregon. Did they ride their horses all that way or did they scrape up train fare? Gram and one of her sisters job hunting in 1895—as if they didn't realize they were Indian women and the limitations that imposed on them. I bet they were all dressed up, too, in job-hunting attire, in corsets and dresses with long skirts and bustles and high-buttoned shoes, trying their damnedest to look presentable.

They knew their grandfather had been named Father of Oregon for all the help he'd given Oregon's pioneers. Lots of help—money and supplies. Once, several big canoes carrying one hundred settlers and their supplies overturned. Those people lost everything they had, and Dr. McLoughlin helped them.

Sometimes he even loaned pioneers livestock that belonged to the company, despite orders not to help. Settlement was not in the best interests of the fur trade. But he did help, because he was kind and because he knew that even if he and the company didn't offer any help at all . . . even if they let the settlers starve or freeze to death . . . that wouldn't stop the settlement of the West. Nothing would.

Gram and her sisters knew all about his acts of kindness and that he had helped the early pioneers, but I doubt that they knew that when Dr. McLoughlin died in 1854, there were many among Oregon's most prominent families who owed him money . . . a great deal of money! Eight pages of promissory notes written by people after whom streets were named in Portland. Eight pages of bad debts totaling eighty thousand dollars. An immense amount of money in 1854.

And McLoughlin's magnificent house, which became Oregon's first museum (the one my mother took me to visit when I was a little girl), was confiscated by the state (along with most of his property) on the grounds that his land claims were made when the Territory was held in joint occupancy (as were everyone else's claims).

McLoughlin had been the representative of that hated British company. Hostilities were not forgotten once the border dispute was settled and Oregon was firmly American. But McLoughlin's many kindnesses and all the money he had loaned the good pioneers *was* forgotten.

The state allowed John and Margaret to live in their house (but not to bequeath it). When Margaret died in 1860, it became the property of the state of Oregon.

Many years later, when both Dr. and Mrs. McLoughlin were long dead, his many kindnesses were remembered at last (though racism lived on, and no bad debts were ever repaid). The beautiful house that had been confiscated by the state became a boarding house for a while. Then it was

a brothel. It was about to be demolished when the Historical
Society rescued it, salvaged it, turned it into Oregon's first
museum. They named Dr. John McLoughlin the Father of
Oregon and had a statue made of him and sent it to Washington, D.C.

But when two young women came along, two poor,
shabby Indian women from somewhere up in Idaho along
the Canadian border, looking for work, they were promptly
dismissed. They seemed to think that they, as granddaughters of the Father of Oregon, deserved some sort of special
consideration. Naive. So unpresentable they were unfit for
any sort of employment . . . save that of washerwomen.

So young Angeline McLoughlin returned to the Kootenay
Valley, where she did not, at least fully, belong either.

Did she ever hate her Indianness? At least sometimes? At
least a little? She knew how unacceptable she was because of
her looks (and maybe even an accent). I tried to recall a
time—was there one?—when I hated my Indianness. Really
hated it, not just been hurt by prejudice, but a time I really
wished I were not, did not have to be, an Indian.

*When I was six or seven years old, at Christ the King Elementary School
in Omak, Washington, a little town adjacent to the Colville Reservation.
Other Indian kids went to the public school, or to the Catholic mission
boarding school. I was the only Indian kid at Christ the King. No
playground equipment there. No swings or slides or teeter-totters. At
recess the nuns organized the kids in hand-holding games like Red Rover
and Drop the Handkerchief and London Bridge Is Falling Down.
Nobody would hold my hand. They refused to touch my brown Indian
hands. Even when the nuns tried to make them.*

I went home after school and filled a white enamel basin with water, then poured a cup of Purex bleach into it and soaked my hands. For a long time. As long as I could. My hateful brown hands. I hoped and prayed I could make them white. That I could make myself acceptable enough.

A year after Angeline's job-hunting expedition to Portland, she married a hard-drinking Irish railroad man from New York City (or County Clare, depending on how you looked at it) and had seven children with skin as presentable as snow. And every one of them married white, had white children. But then something went wrong.

One of Gram's presentable daughters, the girl who had once won an Irish beauty contest, left her white husband. She left her first miserable marriage for a dark man who spoke with an accent. A full-blood. A reservation Indian.

Years later there I was at my grandmother's house. I imagine I stood out among the little towheads who were my second cousins. (When we grew up I would hear my blond cousins tell people, "I'm part Indian," or "I have some Indian blood." Just a little Indian blood. A little is enough. Their great-great-grandmother was an Indian princess, you know).

What did Gram think of, way back then, when she looked at me? At my Indian face, which was rather like her own? Did she remember the trip she and her sister made to Portland in 1895 "seeking employment" (as the Historical Society woman put it) "and *escape* from their unenviable surroundings," which they did not succeed in getting because they were too dark? Their Indian blood. Their Indian looks. No escape. Not then. Not yet. Who did I remind Gram of if not herself?

Return to
Bear Paw

I lived in Seattle in 1986 when Salish-Kootenay Community College (in Western Montana) invited me to do an eight-day speaking tour, sponsored by Salish-Kootenay through a grant from Montana State Council on the Humanities. I went to Montana in May 1986 on a tour that began at the National Indian Youth Conference at the University of Montana in Missoula and took me to four Indian Colleges: Salish-Kootenay, Blackfeet, Rocky Boy and Fort Belknap. I flew from Seattle to Missoula. An employee of SK College, himself a Kootenay Indian, drove me from Missoula to the end of my tour in the eastern part of the state. I had never been to Montana before.

I

Montana was startlingly cold for May, especially compared to the mild drizzle I had just left in Seattle. I didn't bring any cold-weather clothing, no coat, no scarf, no gloves, no shoes except for the open-toed pumps I wore on the airplane. Before I went to sleep the first night, I had a sore throat. When I woke, I had a bad cold that would last the length of my stay in Montana.

Montana was cold and big and desolate, full of empty, wide-open spaces, no greenery, it seemed (compared to Seat-

tle), very few trees. BIG SKY COUNTRY, the license plates pro-
claimed. Nothing blocked the view of the sky, so it seemed
to be bigger than in other places. I kept my speaking engage-
ments, ate in roadside diners, slept in cheap motels, took
liberal doses of my cold remedy and endured. Twangy country western music played everywhere in Montana, seemed to
permeate the crisp mountain air. The cold weather became
even colder. (Hard to believe it was really May.) From the
beginning I longed to be home in Seattle.

I did not come to Montana to make a pilgrimage to the
Bear Paw battleground, to close the circle. I hadn't even
realized, at first, that the place where the cavalry finally
caught up with the Indians led by Chief Joseph was in
Montana. And I hadn't thought of my grandmother, my
father's mother, who had been among those Indians, for
many years.

But now it was impossible not to think of her, not to think
of Chief Joseph and the Great Flight of 1877, for often my
path and the path of those fugitive Indians would cross.
Sometimes a stone or metal "state historical marker" would
mark the spot where a skirmish or some other event had
occurred. Sometimes my driver would point out a certain
place and tell me what had happened there.

Near one small town the army had put a barricade of
timber to stop the Indians. But when dark fell, the nine
hundred and some Indians, including women, children, old
people, with their horses and belongings, slipped up along a
narrow ledge where it didn't seem a mountain goat could go,
up above the heads of the sleeping soldiers, around the white
man's barricade and down the other side.

"Do you know about Chief Joseph and his war with the

government?" asked my driver. I nodded yes. Sure. The government promised Chief Joseph of the Nez Percé he would be allowed to remain in his homeland, the beautiful, fertile Wallowa Valley in Oregon, but then the government took another look and changed its mind. The Wallowa Valley was good land, too good to be Indian land. They told him he would have to remove himself and his people to a seedy, rocky, arid piece of land in Idaho nobody wanted, but Joseph refused to go there. At first, I think, Joseph intended to fight a war. My father told me how it was said he went to all the tribes of the region—the Coeur d'Alene, Kalispell, Spokane, Kootenay—seeking support, but no one would join forces with him. By 1877 the Indian wars in what would become Washington, Idaho, and Oregon had been fought and lost, treaties had been signed. The great power and ruthlessness of the United States government was well understood by then. Fighting another war would be a futile endeavor. And besides, the other tribes did not get as raw a deal as Chief Joseph.

My tribe, the Coeur d'Alene (whose French name, given them in the early 1700s, means "heart of steel"), were never removed from their beautiful ancestral land, only confined to one small corner of it. What the tribes wanted now was peace. No more war. No more bloodshed. No more taking away of land. Chief Joseph and his followers were on their own.

He and his chiefs—Looking Glass, Toolhoolzote and the others—decided they would run away from the United States rather than turn themselves in to the soldiers who had hunted them since they left the Wallowa. They would run to Canada and join the Sioux chief, Sitting Bull, who had been

granted political asylum there after his defeat of Custer and
the 7th Cavalry at the Little Big Horn. The army, led by
General Howard, was relentless in its pursuit of Chief Joseph, but not good at keeping up with Indians. For a while
the 7th Cavalry, seeking revenge after once having been
wiped out by Indians, joined in the chase, but the 7th Cavalry was easily shaken. Four months after the flight began,
the Indians stopped and made camp in the Little Bear Paw
Mountains just thirty miles from the safety of the Canadian
border, unaware that another division, commanded by General Sherman (of Civil War fame), approached from the east.
There Sherman's forces found them, and the last battle
began.

A Nez Percé warrior named Yellow Wolf described his
feelings after the Battle at the Bear Paw had begun, but
before it was over, when they all knew it could only end in
defeat: "I felt the end coming. All for which we had suffered
was lost. Thoughts came of the Wallowa where I grew up,
of my own country when only Indians were there, of teepees
along the bending river, of the blue clear lake, wide meadows with horses and cattle herds. From the mountains and
forests, voices seemed to be calling. I felt as though dream-
ing; not my living self . . . then, with rifle I stood forth, saying
to my heart, 'Here I will die fighting for my people and for
our home!' "

"That place where the last battle was fought," my driver told
me, "is right near your last stop, about twenty miles or so
from Fort Belknap." But it would be late by then, I thought,
and I would still have a trip ahead of me, to Great Falls,
where I would spend the night, then board my plane for

Seattle the next morning. And it was cold and getting colder, and I wasn't feeling well.

"We could go there if you like. To the Bear Paw." My throat still felt raw.

"I don't know," I said. "Maybe. Is there anything there?"

"No. An empty field. A stone monument. Nothing."

"Maybe. Maybe I'll want to go there. I can't say yet. My grandmother was there, you know. She was with those Chief Joseph people."

"Is that so? She was Nez Percé?"

"No. How she happened to be with them had to do with a case of mistaken identity."

When I was four or five, my father told me how it was: My grandmother, a young girl of fifteen or sixteen in the summer of 1877, had been with a group of Coeur d'Alene root gatherers. As was their custom, they had gone quite a distance from Coeur d'Alene country into what used to be Nez Percé territory to dig camas roots. (Camas was dried and stored, used as winter food.) And, as was also their custom whenever they traveled away from their own home, the camas diggers—women, children, old people—had a small group of armed men watching over them as they worked. This was during the time Chief Joseph and his band hid out and evaded the soldiers who tried to find them.

One day while my grandmother and the others dug camas in an open field and warriors watched from hiding places in the hills above, the United States cavalry came riding up.

An army translator spoke in Chinook* asking the root

*Chinook: An Indian trade language.

gatherers to tell them where Chief Joseph was. They were looking for Nez Percé and believed they had found some.

One old man spoke Chinook to the translator, explaining the situation, telling him they were Coeur d'Alene root gatherers, not Nez Percé, and they knew nothing about Chief Joseph. The commander yelled in English, "Liar!" and raised his gun, aimed it at the old man, and told the translator to tell him to take him to Chief Joseph or he would kill him.

The old man said again he didn't know where Chief Joseph was; the commander shot him dead. The warriors swooped down from their hiding places firing their guns, picking off soldiers. Those few Coeur d'Alene killed a good many soldiers that day and beat the rest into retreat. They were a long way from home. They had no choice after that but to find Chief Joseph and join forces with him. That was how it happened that my grandmother, a Coeur d'Alene, was swept along with the Chief Joseph people pursued by Howard, Miles, the 7th Cavalry, and the Great Warrior himself, Sherman, running for her life for the Canadian border and the camp of Sitting Bull.

II

My grandmother, the one who ran with Chief Joseph, died five years before my birth so I have no memories of my own of her. But I heard a lot about her from both my parents, from my uncle and cousins and sisters who did know her and had memories. My three sisters, who are ten, twelve, and fourteen years older than I, remember a little old woman who liked to joke, who told them Indian stories in our Native language. (She never learned English. They knew Indian as children.) How I envied them. How I wished I, too, had known her, had listened to her stories, had understood the language. I imagined her, though, when I was a child, and she became almost real to me.

My family had a photograph of her taken in old age: She is small and thin, her face very wrinkled, her eyes squint in the sun. Her long hair is white. She wears it parted in the middle and in two braids that hang in front to her waist. She is dressed Indian style.

She had a fragile appearance, but she was never fragile, they said, never. She was strong and tough, full of energy and industry, she kept busy. She made her own soap and scented it with pine needles. She went berry picking and she made Indian dishes nobody knows how to make anymore. She sewed all her own clothes. One ongoing activity of hers was the making of beautiful, useful articles: deerskin bags decorated with colored glass beads, cornhusk bags, and these, too, with intricate designs, moccasins, and infant cradle boards. She put them away and kept them sort of in the way young girls once kept a hope chest—for a day that would follow her death and funeral—the feast day when her belongings would be given away to friends and family. She wanted them to have something she made herself by which to remember her.

She was a rider of horses, too, a great rider of horses. She never gave up riding.

Way into old age she would ride, my mother told me, bareback, sometimes long distances. It was twenty miles from their home to the mission village. My grandmother preferred to ride her horse to the village on Sundays rather than go with my parents in their automobile, and she always would if weather permitted. She liked to get an early start, go to an early Mass, eat with friends and relatives, rest, attend a second Mass and visit a bit with her old cronies before heading home. In my mind's eye I can see her riding through the woods and open meadows on Sunday, all decked out in her finery—blue flower-print dress, her long-fringed maroon Spanish trade shawl, a silk scarf tied around her head, riding proud, beautiful, white-haired Indian woman, grandmother I could only know in my mind's eye, in my heart's eye.

My grandmother was a very devout Catholic, as were her parents before her. The conversion of the Coeur d'Alene was in response to an ancient prophecy that said three black ravens would come to them one day bringing the sacred word of the Creator. The ravens would only come when the people were ready to receive the new revelations. In time three Jesuit missionaries, or Black Robes, as they were called, did come, and they were welcomed and listened to. The tribe embraced Catholicism. As practiced by the Coeur d'Alene, it was a rather peculiar brand of Catholicism, and it was not at all "in place of" traditional religious beliefs, but rather an extension of them.

My father's generation, though, was of that first generation born *after* the conquest and the advent of the reservation system, the first generation of Indians to have Christianity forced upon it. The Church, for him, was an instrument of assimilation, an authority sponsored and sanctioned by the government whose primary purpose was to "civilize" the Indian and make him as much like a white man as possible.

My father could recall, for instance, being beaten by a priest at mission school for speaking his own language. He, unlike his mother, was not a devout Catholic. He was, in fact, about as far from a devout Catholic as one could get.

My parents once told me (actually they were retelling each other the story, remembering it, laughing about it, after forty years of marriage) about when they were newlyweds and his mother, who had been living with him prior to his marriage, took extreme measures to get them to marry in the Catholic church.

When my father married my mother and brought her, his new part-white, English-speaking wife home, he told his mother they did not intend to marry in the Church. His mother tried to get him to change his mind, but he would not. His mother could not live with the two of them under the circumstances. She moved out—not to live with another son, as she could have, though. She pitched her tepee in the woods behind the house and lived there.

She used the same well, the same paths they used. They saw her all the time, coming and going, busy around her home. She would not speak to them, nor look at them, nor acknowledge their presence in any way. To her, they were invisible.

They continued to speak to her, to say good morning, how are you, to invite her to go for rides in their automobile, to go into town with them on a hot summer day for some ice cream. But the old lady had a heart of steel. The summer wore on in this way.

One month passed. Then two. My grandmother stead-fastly continued to live in the woods in her tepee. In the end the old lady won, despite my father's feelings about the Church. Before the first frost my parents married in a Catholic ceremony, and my grandmother moved back into the house and stopped pretending they were invisible.

III

The Big Sky Country of Montana, the mountainous terrain, the grey, cold weather, the country western music, the motion of the car took me out of myself and my own petty hardships. (I had a cold, I had to eat in diners and sleep in cheap motels.) I had to speak to nine audiences in eight days (as a single mother I needed the money), though I would rather be home. I recognized these as petty concerns as we made our way across the big, big state of Montana. I saw her, my grandmother, the young girl she had been in 1877, more and more clearly. I drew closer and closer to her. She was there when they drove their ponies and cattle across a treacherous river and over two mountain ranges (they sometimes reached altitudes of ten thousand feet). Always (until that last day) they managed to keep ahead of the soldiers. In the last month they had no more cattle herds and only a few ponies.

Their food supplies ran out. Their clothes and moccasins were worn out. They became ragged, cold and hungry and could not stop to hunt or gather food or make new clothes. They wrapped their bleeding feet in rags and continued. They hurriedly buried their dead in shallow graves along the wayside. Soldiers noted scarred trees where hungry Indians had eaten bark and that they left behind a path marked by blood.

I thought of her, the devout Catholic girl she was, swept along with Nez Percé, who were never the friend of the Coeur d'Alene, whose language was not the same or even similar, whose culture was not her own.

I remembered something I heard about Chief Joseph when I was a child of eleven: he, always portrayed as "noble" in books, films, poems (in *Bury My Heart at Wounded Knee*), had actually been a mean person, a wicked man who hated women and treated them very badly.

My two best friends when I was a girl living on the Yakima Reservation were sisters and they were half Nez Percé. They and their mother were direct descendants of Chief Looking Glass. There was very bad blood between Joseph and Looking Glass (even on that last evening they disagreed). Joseph wanted to let the exhausted people stop and rest at the Bear Paw, then, refreshed, make the thirty miles into Canada in one long march the next day. Looking Glass urged that they push on, despite the belief that no soldiers were near, that they would be safe. They would not be safe, he argued, until they reached Canada. Then they could rest. But Joseph prevailed. Looking Glass, among many others, lost his life at the Bear Paw.

The grandfather of my friends was a grandson of Looking Glass. He said (and his mother, who had been there, told him) that Chief Joseph beat women and worse. On one occasion he had one of his wives put to death because he believed she had brought him bad luck at stick games.*

---

*Stick games: a form of gambling among Indians of the West and the Pacific West. Two teams face each other. Each team has a "hider," who hides a marked bone, and a "guesser," who guesses where the bone is hidden. Sometimes the game is played for high stakes.

Whether or not it is true that Chief Joseph was a misogy-
nist and had had a woman put to death because she brought
him bad luck, I'll never know for sure. But I didn't doubt it
when I heard it at age eleven, and I've read accounts of
Indian chiefs of that region (of an earlier time) having wives
put to death for the same reason. It could be true. At any rate
the Nez Percé, to my grandmother, were strange people with
different beliefs and customs. Maybe their leader held
women in low regard, as the grandson of Looking Glass told
me. They were not in any way *her people*. Except one: they
were Indians and all Indians had in common a powerful
enemy who had conquered them and would now hold them
in captivity and would not tolerate any defiance.

So there she was, a young Catholic Coeur d'Alene, running for her life with Nez Percé (they left a trail marked by
blood) from the United States Army (which was commanded
by a man who was in fact against the reservation system,
who believed Indians should all be killed off lest the government end up supporting "a race of paupers." "The only
good Indian is a dead Indian" was a heartfelt sentiment in
the America of 1877). And where were they going? To Canada to join the Sioux chief, Sitting Bull. And what kind of a
life would she, the little girl who would be my grandmother,
have were they to make good their escape? While the Nez
Percé were never the friend of the Coeur d'Alene, the Sioux,
still polygamous in 1877, were their bitter enemy. The literal
translation of the Coeur d'Alene word for "Sioux" is "cut-
throat."

The last days of the Great Flight were in September, and
that year it was, as it often is, very cold in Montana, maybe
as cold as the time of my own journey. I know it snowed in

the night while they camped and slept in the Little Bear Paw
Mountains. I know the snow fell softly throughout the next
day.

IV

The morning of the last day of my tour I woke in the
predawn hours and looked out the motel-room window and
saw snow. Three or four inches of snow covered the ground,
the rooftops, the cars, weighed heavily upon electrical wires.
Somewhere I heard a radio: country western music at five
A.M. The snow fell hard. It was time to go.

We reached Fort Belnap by noon and found my lecture
there had been canceled. Classes had all been canceled, too,
due to the heavy snowfall that closed the roads in the northern part of the reservation, where most of the students lived.
They were snowed in. I had time now, lots of time. I had
noticed a sign that said, TO THE INDIAN BATTLEGROUND. It was
twenty-odd miles away. That was all. After eight days' time,
all those hours of recalling what I knew about my grandmother and the Great Flight of 1877, and imagining how it
must have been, after traveling all those hard Montana
miles, I felt compelled to complete the journey now, to close
the circle. I asked my driver if, given the snow, it would be
possible to visit the Bear Paw. Would the roads be passable?
Yes, he said. The roads would be fine. If not, we could turn
back. But he thought it would be all right.

Those twenty-odd miles were hard ones. The wind blew
and the snow drifted across the narrow winding road as we

climbed higher and higher. Sometimes the road would be entirely hidden by snowdrifts.

The car was small, and I felt our vulnerability, should something go wrong. But my driver was used to bad weather and lonely stretches of country road. This probably wasn't even bad weather to him. Just a light spring snowfall.

Cattle lined up against the fence alongside the road, their white faces watching us. "It's as though they heard we were coming through," I said, "and all turned out to watch us pass."

"Maybe," he said, "they heard you were disappointed because you didn't see any buffalo in Montana and came to act as stand-ins. Actually that's what they do when they know a storm is coming."

"Why?"

"I don't know."

I sat back and watched the snow fall as we passed through this desolate area. We passed no house along the way, no filling station. We didn't even pass any other cars on the road. After what seemed like a long time my driver pulled over and stopped the car.

"Here we are," he said.

We climbed out of the car into the snow, four or five inches deep. I slipped and almost fell. My shoes, my thin high-heeled pumps, filled with snow, and snow fell on my hair and clothes and melted. I clutched my long red cardigan sweater close to me. It didn't keep me warm.

How quiet it was now that the car's engine no longer ran. No sound of wind or birds calling or human voices, only the quiet of the softly falling snow.

"There"—he indicated the mountains in the distance,

barely visible through the veil of falling snow—"is Canada."
Their destination.

We walked over to the monument, a bronze plate set in
stone. On the plate, in relief, were two figures: one a soldier
in uniform, presumably General Howard; the other an Indian, naked from the waist up, presumably Chief Joseph.
Below the figures, also in relief, the words FROM WHERE THE
SUN NOW STANDS I WILL FIGHT NO MORE FOREVER. The last
words of Joseph's surrender speech.

"Look at this," he said, lightly touching the figure of the
Indian. I touched it too. Some kind of blemishes . . . deep
scratches on the figure of the Indian.

"What is this?"

"Bullet nicks," he answered. It took a moment for it to
sink in, to imagine good old boys up here drinking beer and
getting in a little target practice and expressing themselves.
After all these years Indians aren't generally very popular in
Montana. FROM WHERE THE SUN NOW STANDS, it said. I WILL
FIGHT NO MORE . . ., and there were bullet-nicks, . . . FOREVER,
on the bronze monument. FROM WHERE THE SUN, depicting
the peace-making SUN NOW STANDS . . ., the final surrender,
I WILL FIGHT . . ., after the slaughter, NO MORE. . . . They
shot only at FOREVER, the Indian. Not the soldier. Bullet
nicks.

We stood on a rise above what I realized had to be the
battleground. "There it is," he said, "down here." Yes.

The Indians had come far, had suffered such great hardships, were so tired and hungry. There would be time
enough, or so they thought, to stop for the night, their last
night. They knew of Howard, a good long distance away,
and they knew they had completely lost the other, the 7th

Cavalry. But they were not aware of a third division, which now came towards them from the east. So they went down there, made their camp in the gulch beside Snake Creek. They hunted, cooked their fresh meat, ate and rested. What did that girl dream of that night as she lay sleeping? Did she dream of the beautiful Coeur d'Alene country that was her home? Did she see the faces of her father and mother? Or did she now dream of her new life in Canada?

The cavalry attacked just before dawn while the Indians still slept. The battle raged as the snow fell, hour after bloody hour, throughout most of the day. When the Battle at the Bear Paw ended, 419 Indians—88 men, 184 women and 147 children—lay dead on the frozen ground.

"Do you want to go down there?" he asked me. I said no. Not in those shoes. Not dressed as I was. I wouldn't be able to take the cold much longer. He went alone. My ears ached in the cold, and my feet felt as though they would turn to ice. I saw him brush the snow from the markers for the communal grave. He stayed there awhile, kneeling in the snow.

The cold reached my bones, yet I stood in the snow and felt myself being in that place, that sacred place. I saw how pitifully close lay the mountains of Canada. I felt the biting cold. I was with those people, was part of them. I felt the presence of my grandmother there as though two parts of her met each other that day: the ghost of the girl she was in 1877 (and that part of her will remain forever in that place) and the part of her that lives on in me, in inherited memories of her, in my blood and in my spirit.

At length the spell broke. I could take the cold no longer. I went back to the car, to the relative warmth and comfort there.

My driver joined me in five or ten minutes. He started the engine, breaking the silence. The tires spun in the mud, but just a bit. Then we pulled forward, made a circle and turned back onto the road, which was easier to travel going down.

The snow stopped, turned to rain. We didn't talk much the rest of the way to the highway and then to Great Falls. The day grew dim.

Chief Joseph of the Nez Percé was thirty-six years old at the time of the Battle at the Bear Paw. His surrender speech was made through an interpreter and recorded on the spot by an army clerk. It would become one of the most famous of American speeches:

"Tell General Howard I know his heart. What he told me before I have in my heart. I am tired of fighting. Our chiefs are killed. Looking Glass is dead. Toolhoolzote is dead. The old men are all dead. It is cold and we have no blankets. The little children are freezing to death. My people, some of them, have run away to the hills and have no blankets, no food; no one knows where they are—perhaps freezing to death. I want to have time to look for my children and see how many of them I can find. Maybe I shall find them among the dead. Hear me, my chiefs! From where the sun now stands I will fight no more forever."

After it was all over, my grandmother would return to Coeur d'Alene country in northern Idaho. She would live through a smallpox epidemic that would wipe out most of the tribe, begun when the Coeur d'Alene people, no longer permitted to go to Montana to hunt buffalo, were given smallpox-infected army blankets.

She would marry a tall, shrewd Coeur d'Alene man, who would, as a rancher, provide very well for her and the six sons and one daughter they would have together.

She would give birth to my father in the mountains one summer day in 1892 while out picking huckleberries. She would tell him about his birth in the mountains and how she came riding down with the basket strapped to her horse on one side filled with huckleberries and the basket on the other side containing her new baby boy.

My father would go to mission school at the age of twelve, where he would learn English: to read, to write, to speak. He would become a soldier in the United States Army during World War I (though Indians would not be made citizens until 1924). He would marry and have one son. His first wife would die. He would marry my mother when he was thirty-nine years old, and they would have four daughters together.

My paternal grandmother would live to be a very old woman, and she and my three older sisters would know each other very well. She would tell them stories, speaking the old language they would understand as children but forget as adults (and I would never know).

The old woman who survived the Great Flight and the Battle at the Bear Paw and the smallpox epidemic would die peacefully in her sleep in her home in Idaho in 1941.

I would be born five years later in 1946, shortly after the end of World War II. And though I would live on that same Idaho reservation, and then on the Yakima in Washington State, I would grow up knowing only the English language. I would go to college and law school. Eventually I would become a writer. As a writer I would go back to that hard Montana country, and on a cold day in May 1986, I would, at last, return to the Bear Paw.

Dust
to
Dust

A summer day in 1976. My son and daughter (they are twelve and five) and I are swimming at Lake Coeur d'Alene. They've only known the San Francisco Bay area before now, the only swimming they've done has been in a crowded municipal pool. Both are very taken with this area: the mountains, clear lakes, evergreen trees—the plentitude of space. We've had a good day here. It's late afternoon. "I wish this day would last forever," my little daughter says, floating on her back in the water. Nothing disturbs the calm.

"Nothing lasts forever," my son says. "Not this day, not us, not this lake, those mountains. Not even the sun up in the sky." I give him a dirty look. "Well, it doesn't," he says. "Nothing lasts."

Not that day or that summer or that year. Not the marriage I had then. Not their childhood. Not my youth. All that is gone now (though the lake, mountains and sun are still there).

May 1992. My son lives in California. I seldom see him. My daughter is a student in southern Idaho (some five hundred miles from Spokane). I live in New York with my third husband. My daughter and I are coincidentally in Spokane at the same time: she to attend her friend's wedding, I to interview for a one-year appointment at Eastern Washington University.

I rent a car, and when the interviewing process is over (I was offered and accepted the appointment at Eastern Washington as Distinguished Visiting Writer for next term), my daughter and I head out to the reservation, which is, as I recall, only a little more than an hour's drive from Spokane, just a little northeast. I want to visit my father's grave, because I haven't been there in fifteen years and because 1992 marks the one hundredth anniversary of his birth. I want to remember him and those he descended from and my own time (which ended when I was ten) living in my ancestral land. I want to share these memories with my daughter.

I am surprised, though, to find that I've forgotten the way. I should know it . . . it looks so familiar . . . and yet. I stop at the Idaho Visitor's Information Center and Rest Stop just east of the city of Coeur d'Alene. The girl behind the counter is helpful. She shows me on a road map, marks it and gives it to me. There, right there is the Coeur d'Alene Indian Reservation. "Where are you folks from?" she asks, smiling like an airline stewardess.

"Actually," I answer, "I'm from here. But it's been a long time. I live in New York now." The girl makes a face at the mention of New York.

"Do you like it in New York? I'm from Brooklyn myself." I can't help noticing there's no trace of a Brooklyn accent. "This is much better. I just love it here. Just love it!" And with that she turns to help another disoriented tourist. This area is full of newcomers these days, refugees from densely populated regions of the country, mostly Los Angeles and New York. They all "just love it here," it seems. We get back in my rented car and hit the road. I know my way now. I don't need to look at the map.

The last time my daughter and I were together was Christmas break when she met her stepfather and visited New York for the first time. We rode subway trains, climbed the stairs to the top of the Statue of Liberty, saw a Broadway show and much more. Those were a busy two weeks. This time we have just one day. This will be a much different kind of visit.

"When I was a little girl, my family lived in Idaho on our tribe's reservation. We drew our water from a well. We lit our house with kerosene lamps. We had an outhouse. I rode a little yellow school bus to school."

I remember telling my daughter these things when she was little. She asked for details. I could recall some: "I used to catch frogs down by the creek. I'd play with them as though they were dolls, give them names, have them act out stories. When I was through playing with them, I would take them back to the creek. After a time they got so used to me, I wouldn't even have to try to catch them anymore. They would just let me pick them up. They would hop right on my head and shoulders. I think they enjoyed being my dolls and looked forward to playing.

"My uncle (my father's brother) and his family lived about ten miles away from us (we all lived way out on the reservation—very isolated). One winter evening we went to visit them, and while we were there, it began to snow. A blizzard came up, and we got snowed in for days. I was about four, I think. It was a terrible blizzard. My uncle's family lived in the house that my father's father had built a long time ago,

where my father and uncle had grown up. It was so big and
old . . . so sprawling. So cold. They closed off all the rooms
except for the kitchen and big living room. All of us—about
eight altogether—had to sleep in the one room in order to
keep warm. Some slept on pallets on the floor. I remember
I slept in a single bed with my mother.

"Every evening we would ask Dad and Uncle to tell Coyote stories, but they would refuse. Not until the temperature
dropped to its lowest point, they said. Because telling Coyote
stories could cause the weather to change drastically, and
they didn't want to take a chance on its changing for the
worse. When the temperature hit forty degrees below zero,
they decided it couldn't get any colder. 'Forty below,' they
said, 'Forty below. That's it. Coyote stories tonight.' Then
they began. Every evening (I think there were only about
three until the snowplows came and cleared the roads and
freed us to go home) from then on we had a Coyote festival.

"Coyote is an outrageous character that all Indian tribes
of the West told stories about. No, not like in Road Runner
cartoons. Not that stupid. And not that single-minded either.
And not a failure, at least not always. He had no scruples,
none at all. He would tell his kids, 'Look at that!' and while
their heads were turned, he would steal food from their
plates. He lied and swindled and took advantage of everyone. Once, when he got tired of chasing rabbits, he pretended he was dying and wanted the rabbit chief and his
people to come to his tepee so he could apologize to them for
killing so many rabbits and making their lives miserable for
so many years. He wanted to die with a clear conscience. So
the rabbit chief came, and Coyote lay there all weak and
pitiful and said how his soul was tortured because of the sort

of life he'd lived. The rabbit chief forgave him—they all
did—and told him he could die in peace. Coyote said,
'Come closer, please. I want to tell you more.' His voice was
so weak. They drew closer. Then he signaled his kids with his
eyes, and they closed the exit tight, and Coyote jumped up
and clubbed the rabbits to death. He had enough food to last
awhile. He wouldn't have to go chasing rabbits for weeks.
Sometimes the stories were hilarious. Sometimes he got his
just desserts. Like the time he believed the sun's job was easy
and he got the sun to trade places for a day. As Coyote (now
the sun) moved across the sky high above the earth, he
looked down and saw all kinds of goings-on. He knew everyone's secrets and, being the sort of person he was, he was not
about to keep his mouth shut. He ridiculed them and
laughed at them and told all their secrets. But he did himself
in because he saw himself and revealed his own embarrass-
ing secrets and the next day had to take his own place again
and live with being the butt of everyone's jokes for a very
long time."

My daughter loved those Coyote stories when she was
little and the stories I told her about my childhood. I painted
a pretty picture for her—we had such good things to eat
when we lived in Idaho. "My mother baked her own bread.
We would go up into the mountains and pick huckleberries.
She would make huckleberry jam. Oh, and wild-currant
preserves. Dad would hunt. Pheasant and deer . . . deer meat
is called venison. Mom and her old best friend and sister-in-
law would go fishing at the lake. Trout, perch, sunfish. We
had chickens when I was very little. Then we didn't for a
long time. I was the last one to try to raise chickens. My dad
gave me ten baby chicks as an Easter present. Were those

chicks ever cute. Ten little roosters. Then, one night when they were adolescents (they had tiny red combs on top of their heads and real feathers but still hadn't lost all of their yellow fluff), a weasel tunneled under the wall of the chicken house. When I went out to feed them the next morning, they were gone. All that was left of them was a little spot of blood and a little white feather on the ground."

This was all true. Not one word, not one incident was a lie. It was just not the whole truth. We moved around so much—mostly because of my mother's habitual running away, but for other reasons too. My middle sister's illness. A time or two we went with my father when he had a construction job. We always went back to Idaho. But not to the same house. We lived in one house twice, though. When I was little, it had no electricity, and we had to use kerosene lamps. Later, when I was nine, it did have electricity (but still no running water). Then we had a radio and television, and my mother had an old-fashioned wringer washing machine. We still had an outhouse. Still had to heat water on top of the kitchen stove and take baths in a washtub. I went the last few months of second grade in Plummer, Idaho. I skipped third grade that fall and began fourth. We moved. I went back to third. Omak. Fife. Spokane. Round and round. Then back to Idaho again by the time I was in fourth grade again. "We lived out on the reservation the year Elvis Presley became famous. I think I was nine, almost ten, the first time I heard him. Oh, I had such a crush on him, such a crush, and it lasted a long time. I was certain that somehow, when I grew up, I would marry him. I never told anyone about my crush, but I guess it must have been obvious because my parents took me to see Elvis's first film, *Love Me Tender*, for my eleventh birthday. Fourth grade, which I was in that last year on our reservation, was the only grade I ever did entirely at one school. That summer we moved to Tacoma, Washington, and never lived in Idaho again."

I stitched together a happy childhood for myself, an expurgated version I could recall to my little girl. It had order. It had continuity. And it was not a lie. I think I must have made it up for myself first, long before I told it to her—smoothed off the rough edges. And tried to believe in it. I had had a home. I had a place where I belonged, really belonged. I came from a family that valued me.

The day is an extraordinarily beautiful one (and so was the day before and the day before that—all the days while I've been in the area). Everyone comments on the weather, how bright and gorgeous it is after a long winter and harsh early spring. I've been gone from the West for three years, and for me therefore the weather and the great western landscape is more than just "beautiful." In a way it seems that I am seeing it for the first time. Though I'm not used to mountainless terrain and heavy, humid air and hazy skies that only get blue for a handful of days a year, I have not experienced this, actually, in what seems like a long, long time. Compared with what I come from this is paradise. I have hungered for the sight, the presence, of snowcapped mountains (maybe the mountains more than any other aspect, since I've lived near them most of my life until New York. When I first left the West, I dreamed of mountains for weeks—maybe longer). The air is crisp and clean, and the colors are intensely vivid—yellow wheat, blue sky, many shades of green grass, shrubs and trees—even the plain, near-black plowed earth seems intense, deep and rich. One New Yorker who vacationed in the West told me, "The colors out there seem artificial. How could anything natural be that clear and bright—like a Van Gogh painting or something." The air is so fresh-smelling, too, easy to breathe, a pleasure to breathe.

Almost anywhere in the West would seem like this to me, I suppose. But I'm not just anywhere—not at all—I'm home.

I saw myself going home, visiting my father's grave at the tribal cemetery, recalling the time of my childhood. I should have my daughter with me, I thought, especially after she called me to ask details concerning family history and the origin of my family name: "Didn't you tell me that Campbell is actually derived from an Indian name—an anglicized version of your grandfather's name or something?" (The name, Cole-man-née, was my great-grandfather's name. He was born about 1820. We cannot trace our Coeur d'Alene ancestry back any further than him.) She had an assignment to write a paper based on nonlibrarial research and she'd chosen to write about our family history.

Now that she has an interest in such things, now that she's grown, I thought, I should take her home with me. Show her where I used to live. Tell her what I know of what used to be. Pass down what I know to her. Maybe even something of the feeling for the land. She'll remember now.

A few miles from the city of Coeur d'Alene, just before the village (of about eight hundred people) of Plummer, Idaho, we pass a road sign that announces, NOW ENTERING THE COEUR D'ALENE INDIAN RESERVATION. We're home now.

For an Indian, home is the place where your tribe began.

(For some, for my tribe, that place is also where the tribe continued to live after the land was made a reservation.) Home is the place where your people began, and maybe where your family began and your family still is.

The region in eastern Washington and the panhandle of northern Idaho known as the Inland Empire—the cities of Spokane and Coeur d'Alene, the several reservations and all the small cities and towns adjacent to them—has been tribal country for at least a thousand years, most likely longer than that.

I have never heard a creation myth from my own tribe, probably because of their early conversion to Catholicism. (An Indian creation myth would contradict the one I was told about God creating Adam to live in the Garden of Eden and then, while he slept, taking one of his ribs and making Eve.) Most Indian myths tell of tribal people being created in the same place that had been their home for countless generations.

My great-grandfather had no white man's name. It was Cole-man-née. We know because it appears on my grandfather's baptismal certificate. Colemannée, in English, means "dust." The true meaning would have had to do with a significant incident in his life, most likely a brave deed. The word *dust* was meant to remind him and others of the deed. Maybe he dove into the dust to save himself and other people as enemy bullets or arrows whizzed by. Maybe, while a small number of unprotected Coeur d'Alenes were out gathering berries or something, they had seen enemy riding in the distance (U.S. cavalry soldiers, or maybe Lakota or Crow) and, since there was no hiding place and they didn't have a chance of winning if they had to fight, he had covered himself and the others with dust and they had kept very still and invisible as the enemy passed by. Maybe it was dust in a figurative rather than literal sense. It could be anything. Nobody is alive who remembers. I didn't think to ask when it could have been remembered. All I know is that the name Campbell is derived from my great-grandfather's name, Colemannée.

My grandparents, Pauline and Gideon, were the first in my family to have Christian names. Gideon was born in 1853. His surname was Camille on his baptismal certificate, but in the mouths of the American settlers it became Camel and then Campbell. Somehow Gideon came to be called Peter, which he preferred. The name Peter Campbell is on his tombstone. He never learned English, and neither did his wife. They and their contemporaries had to cope with the Indian wars and advent of the reservation. Peter Campbell somehow did cope and became a successful rancher and in the 1880s became our tribe's first judge. His court was one of the first tribal courts in the country.

My father, whose name was Campbell all of his life, was of the first generation born on reservation land, after the Indians had become a conquered people.

We don't know the exact date of my father's birth, but we know it was in summer because his mother had gone up into the mountains to pick huckleberries. A summer day in 1892. When she came down, the basket strapped to her horse on one side was full of huckleberries. The basket on the other side contained her new baby boy.

For my paternal grandparents' generation the white-man's religion was not a bitter thing. It was not even, in whole, a white-man's religion. An old prophecy had it that "three black ravens" would come to the people. Three Jesuit missionaries (or Black Robes) did come to the Coeur d'Alene one day, clamining they brought the word of God. The Coeur d'Alene embraced Catholicism and practiced it as an extension of their traditional religion, which the early missionaries seemed to respect.

But for my father's generation Catholicism was a different matter. The government policy, after the Indian wars were over, was to assimilate the Indian into mainstream American culture . . . to educate the Indian, to beat the Indianness out of him, to do away with everything having to do with the traditional culture that had been. Different churches were contracted to do this. In this region, where the Catholic church already had a toehold, of course it was the Catholics who got the government contract and who established a mission school. My father went to that mission school when he was twelve years old (I don't know how he managed to avoid it for such a long time). There he learned to speak English and to read and write. He was forced to wear shoes. They cut his hair short, and he wore it that way for the rest of his life.

Dad (like all Indian students) was beaten for speaking his own language and for acting too Indian at mission school. Once, when he first went there and still didn't know a word of English, he was put into a dark, windowless space above the chapel in the church building. The opening was boarded up and nailed closed. He didn't know if they would let him out at all. He thought he might die there . . . suffocate or die of thirst or starve to death. It seemed to him that they kept him there a long, long time. He never did find out why they

did that to him, though he did of course understand that he
was being punished.

Dad was never a good Catholic. He was never a good
white-man's Indian. But it was too late to turn back.

I know my way around the reservation. I know it perfectly.
Almost. I drive down by the lake first. I don't want to get out
or anything. I just want to see it, to drive past.

Lake Chatcolet was part of the original land settlement,
but it no longer belongs to us. The government did not,
however, take it away. The tribe lost it in a rather unique
way. In 1908 the tribe gave it to the state of Idaho on the
condition that it and the land surrounding it be maintained
as a state park for the enjoyment of all. Heyburn State Park,
the terms of the gift stipulated, was never to be sold or leased
to private parties. "If this condition is ever violated, owner-
ship of Lake Chatoclet and the surrounding area known as
Heyburn State Park shall revert to the Coeur d'Alene tribe
of Indians."

Of course the state immediately began to sell property and
to issue hundred-year leases. Now it is a developed resort
area. Twenty years ago the tribe brought a lawsuit to have
the property returned. This has strained white-Indian relations in the area, which were never good to begin with. Lots
of wealthy white people own summer homes along the shore
of the lake, and the resort industry is the only one that exists
here. The Indian claim is seen as a threat by many. A federal
court finally ruled in favor of the tribe, but said return of the
land would be too great a penalty and ordered the state to

make a cash settlement. The tribe refused to accept the ruling. The legal battle goes on. Race relations become more strained. The New Aryan Brotherhood has moved into the area.

"Do you remember," I ask my daughter, "when I was going to take you and your brother to swim at my family's old spot?"

"When I was little? Yes. I remember. What happened? I know we didn't swim. You got lost, wasn't that it? You couldn't find it?"

"At first I thought I was lost. But I couldn't find it because it wasn't there."

"Oh, yeah. The land was leveled or something . . . and it had picnic tables and toilets and barbecue pits."

And I'd been telling my children how my family and my dad's brother's family used to go to a certain spot down by the lake that was so perfect. We had to park our cars and go down a steep hill, hanging on to brush and roots of trees. We sometimes had a box of picnic goodies that had to be handed down, not carried. The sand down there wasn't really sand but very fine pebbles, sort of white-and-salmon-colored, and the water was crystal clear. My son, especially, had been looking forward to swimming there. That place was gone though. It no longer exists. Like a lot of other things.

I drive to Worley, which is still very small. Now the streets are paved. There've been a lot of changes. I take my daughter to show her the house where we lived when my father made a swing for me on a big, old tree in the backyard. The house was on the side of a hill right on the last street of the town. Behind our house was a grassy slope and then just forest. We didn't live there for long. I don't remember where we lived before or where we lived after. We lived in five different houses on this reservation.

I find that street, I find that slope, but the house is gone. I can't even tell exactly where our house used to be.

"It doesn't really matter," I tell her. She nods. I stop the car for a moment, but don't shut off the engine. I can't tell. I just can't tell.

I am remembering, but I don't tell her (though I do think I told her before. When she got older, I wanted her to know what kind of childhood I'd had), that night I stowed away in my father's car and went to Canada with him. We lived in the house that had once been on the side of that hill then.

My parents were fighting because my father wanted to drink and my mother refused to buy for him. Indians couldn't legally buy or drink alcohol in the United States until 1954. I was five years old, so it was 1951 at the time. My mother, who could easily pass for white, had bought for him, but not for a very long time. I don't think she ever did during my lifetime. She just refused to do it anymore. She complained about money, he said, but this was her fault, because he had just two choices: buy from a white bootlegger or go to Canada. Either way it would mean a lot of money. I knew when they began to fight that she would not budge and that he would proceed to go on "a bender." She had an ordinarily uneven disposition. She could be really intense when he was gone drinking. He was easygoing most of the time. He was downright jolly when he drank. That's when he would sing and play games with me, give me quarters. I decided to go with him rather than stay home with her.

I went out and got into the backseat of the car and lay

down on the floor. Soon he came bounding out of the house and jumped into the car. We were gone in a cloud of dust. I didn't make my presence known until we were too far away for him to do much about it.

I had a good time in Osoyoos, Canada, where the tavern that catered to American Indians was. There were lots of Indian kids waiting in cars parked in front of the tavern. We got out of our cars and bummed change from the drunks going in and coming out of the tavern. The owner of the tavern would let us come inside to buy candy, soda pop and comic books. We had a roaring good time. After the tavern closed, Dad and I slept in the car. He covered me with his jacket and himself with a newspaper.

The next day we ate at a café, and he had a little more to drink. I kept telling him let's go home, let's go home and then, finally, late in the day, we headed back.

By the time we got to Worley, it was dark. Dad had no intention of going home. He stopped on the main street and told me to get out and walk home. I said no. He reminded me that I'd walked that distance many times, which was true, but it had always been in the daylight, and only once I'd been alone. And then a dog had attacked me.

It still looks like a long way for a little girl to walk alone. Especially in the dark. I turn and drive down that street. Still the same street. I don't remember what it had looked like then, except that it was graveled.

"Why are you driving so slow, Mom? People are looking at us."

"I'm just remembering this street. A dog attacked me on this street one day. It was the first time I'd ever walked to the store and back alone. The dog and his owner were behind a wire fence. The dog growled at me in a very threatening manner, bared his teeth to me. I stopped in my tracks. I was very scared because just one year before, when I was four and we lived in Tacoma, near Cushman Indian Hospital, a dog had bitten me. That dog was the kind that has hair in its eyes. I'd only been trying to brush his hair out of his eyes so he could see. He bit me on the hand. See the scar. I'd had to have my hand stitched up and then, worst of all, I had to go back to the hospital and have a shot every day for a time. A horrible experience. After that I was always afraid of dogs.

"So a year later a dog was growling at me on this street as I was passing by, and his owner smiled and said, 'Don't be frightened, little girl. He likes to bark and growl, but he won't bite. Honest.' So I very warily started walking again, and then, quick as a wink, that big dog jumped over the fence and knocked me down in the gravel. My dress was all dirty and torn and I skinned my elbow, but his owner stopped him before he could bite me. Terrifying. It was terrifying."

The dog had knocked me down on the street and scared me just weeks before the night my dad refused to drive me up this street to our house. I begged him. He could drive away real fast, I told him, before Mom had a chance to say anything. He wouldn't go for it. And he refused to take me with him. He wasn't through drinking. When he drank, drinking was really all he cared about.

I begged and cried and hung on to my father's sleeve, hung on to the door handle, "Please, Daddy, no. Don't make me get out. The dogs. I'm scared of the dogs. The dogs are gonna bite me," but he forced me out and drove away and left me standing there all by myself. There was nothing I could do but try to walk home.

It was dark and cold. I walked very, very slowly, trying not to make any noise on the gravel, thinking if I didn't, maybe the dogs wouldn't know I was there. All around me dogs barked in the dark and seemed to be drawing closer. This time there would be no owners to save me. Sometimes I stood perfectly still, not moving a muscle until the barking ceased, then proceeded, very, very slowly. All the way home—and it still looks like a long distance to me now--the barking dogs followed. I made it home after a very long time. My mother heard my footsteps on the front steps, turned on the light and came down. I had been crying all the way home, I'm sure I must have been dirty. She picked me up and carried me inside. She had been worried sick, she said. She was raving angry at Dad for taking me away. I must learn to stay away from him, she said. Don't go with him again, under any circumstances, when he was drinking. He wasn't to be trusted when he was drinking. I realized that she was right. (She didn't know that I had stowed away of my own free will. I never did tell her. She always thought he took me away.) She fed me and bathed me, put me in a pair of clean pajamas and tucked me in bed.

We reach the end of the street I had had to walk along that night so many years ago. (Worley still has a lot of dogs.) I make a right turn on the main street, and we're out of town.

Miles and miles down the road, way out on the reservation, I find one of the houses we used to live in. We never lived in one that belonged to us (not here on the reservation), though the others did, before I was born. I'm confused. It's so confusing. Another house, my favorite location, has been gone some twenty years. It's all over. All over. And the day is wearing on. I turn back and drive to the mission, or De

Smet—the community that grew up around the Catholic church and the mission school. De Smet is in a little valley. On the highest hill, to the left as you turn off the highway . . . are the church buildings and what is now the tribal school, owned and operated by the tribe. Coeur d'Alene history and Coeur d'Alene language are taught in that school. The church where I made my first Confession, and took my first Communion, where my father's funeral Mass was held, is still there. The old church, where my parents married, where my sisters and I were all baptized, has been gone for a long time. I can just barely remember it. The gymnasium is gone now . . . where all the basketball games, and political meetings and parties and dances were held. And talent shows. I remember those talent shows. That was in the days before anyone had a television. If you lived by the mission, though, you had radio.

On the flat land between this hill where the church buildings stand and the other, is a village of about a hundred houses (all new prefabs) and a general store and post office. These streets are all paved now. We lived at the mission one winter—I don't know why—I don't know why we lived in so many places. I never knew. When we lived there, the streets were dirt. Just dirt. And in the spring the dirt became mud and people laid boards down on the mud so they would have something to walk on. That Easter my mother sent away to Sears Roebuck for a yellow silk dress for me—it was so beautiful—and new white stockings and black patent-leather shoes with straps and buckles. I was so afraid I was going to slip and fall in the mud, but I didn't. Oh, and a hat too (Catholics still had to wear hats or scarves to church if they were girls or women . . . they had to keep their heads covered). My Easter hat was straw with a ribbon that tied under my chin and some fake berries on top . . . red ones with green stems and leaves. The houses in the village then were really poor looking, none of them painted, all weathered a dark brown. Every house had an outhouse.

To the right of the village a road leads up another hill to the cemetery. That's where we're going now.

There are still woods around it, but the cemetery has changed. So neat and manicured. There must be a full-time caretaker or maintenance person. I'm amazed. Not what I expected. The whole reservation, in fact, looks prosperous compared to how it used to look. In Plummer there are Indian-owned businesses now: a supermarket and a garage-filling station, an auto-parts store, a deli. They seem to be doing very well.

"People used to take care of their own family graves," I tell my daughter, "or nobody did. I came here so many times with Dad. He would bring water along. He would work on the graves for hours, weeding them, tidying up." I park the car and we get out. I go to the place where I think our family plot is, but I'm wrong. I can't find it. For the second time today I've lost my way.

"I'll help you find it, Mom. Tell me what to look for. What are some of the names?" I tell her to look for one tall, very fancy headstone—my grandparents' headstone—they were the first ones in our family to be buried here. The other graves around theirs have plain stones. My father's is just a slab. White marble. The Veterans paid for it. A government headstone. I didn't remember the cemetery being this big. It takes twenty minutes to find my family's plot, right on the very edge, overlooking the land.

"Here it is. See . . . this is Dad's grave. You don't remember at all being here before?" She shakes her head no. "You were five. You went around looking for interesting rocks, filling your pockets with rocks."

"I remember I used to do that a lot. Collect rocks."

"Yeah. And you were just singing away as you went about your rock gathering."

There's still space, at the very edge of the plot, for a few more graves. We sit there in the green grass and look out over the land below. We have a sweeping view.

I remember the day my father was buried in 1969. The day of the first moon landing. I had just completed my first hard year of college, had just been accepted at the university. I was slightly older than my own daughter is now. She seems so young to me. Hardly more than a kid, just beginning her life. I hadn't been young. I didn't think of myself as young. Even now, as I look back, I don't seem to have been young in those days.

It was March and, here in Idaho, bitter, bitter cold. Frozen snow covered the ground. A shock to me, coming as I did from sunny California. (I'd left my four-year-old son with his father's parents in California and went alone to my parents' home.) A man I had known for several years but had just begun dating about a month before my father's death gave me the money to buy a plane ticket. I didn't even own a coat at the time. In California I didn't need one. I borrowed a coat from one of my nieces, my oldest sister's oldest daughter who was then a seventeen-year-old high school senior, five years younger than myself. That sister had had to borrow money from me—fifty-some dollars. I don't know how it was that I, who lived on almost nothing for a year while attending college, had any money to loan, but I did. Maybe it was because I had moved to a cabin at Stinson Beach, a sort of resort motel, in the interim between the end of City College's semester and the beginning of the University of California's new quarter, where I was cleaning and painting cabins, weeding flower gardens, helping the owner to prepare for the coming summer-vacation season in exchange for rent. Maybe that was why I had some money . . . welfare money which I did not have to spend on rent. Maybe my boyfriend had loaned it to me. Anyway I had a little money, and I loaned it to my sister so she could pay for two motel rooms in Plummer for herself and her daughters and Mom.

My father's body lay in an open casket at the community hall. His wake would last just one day and one night. A few of his old friends and relatives, my youngest sister and her husband and I would sit up through the night with the body (as is the custom for the family of the deceased).

That evening, as I sat visiting with the relatives and tribal members who had come, one of my nieces told me my oldest sister and her daughter were leaving and were taking the coat they'd loaned me with them. I looked, and there they were, my sister and her daughter, just a few feet from the door and walking fast.

I called to them, but they didn't stop. I had to run to catch up to them, calling their names (I thought they hadn't heard me). They must have forgotten they'd loaned me the coat. Here it was so horribly cold, and I didn't even have a sweater or wrap of any kind. I remember smiling, telling them, believing still . . . after all my sisters had done to me all of my life . . . that they had taken the coat by mistake. *Of course they hadn't.* They had taken it deliberately and most certainly did intend to leave me stranded in the cold with nothing to cover myself. They were angry—outraged—because I'd carelessly draped my niece's coat over the back of a chair where one of my youngest sister's rowdy young children might knock it on the floor. I humiliated myself: "Oh, I'm sorry." Apologizing. Begging. Promising I'd take better care of the damned coat. They very reluctantly handed it back, then went to their motel to sleep. I don't recall whether or not my oldest sister ever repaid that fifty-some dollars.

I do remember that three chairs had been placed beside the grave that morning—not *four* (my mother, who was confined to a wheelchair, was unable to manage getting through the ice and snow so sat waiting inside a car during the graveside service). My three sisters sat in those chairs. Their children and I stood behind them creating a wall against the hard, bitter wind. I remember my shoes were thin-soled pumps with little heels. As I stood on the frozen snow, the cold passed through those shoes as though they weren't there. The biting wind passed through my niece's precious navy-blue spring coat the same way.

The graveside service seemed to last a long time. Some old men from the Veterans of Foreign Wars fired their guns in salute into the sky, and the shots echoed like thunder over the hills. Afterward they took the American flag off my father's coffin and folded it in the official military fashion, then presented it to my oldest sister, who later gave it to my mother. A few more words were said. The coffin was lowered into the grave. It caught on the sides, and some men had to jump down there and sort of kick it free and into the grave. Then everyone filed past and threw a handful of dirt onto the coffin. Then I gave my niece her coat and got into my middle sister's car for the ride back to Wapato.

And I came back to this cemetery once, in 1976, with my two children. And now here I am today in the spring of 1992.

"What are you thinking about, Mom?"

"The day we buried my father. It was so cold. So very, very cold."

"I know. And you had no coat of your own."

"That's right. I didn't even have a coat of my own."

"Mom?"

"Yeah?"

"Mom, I'm glad you got out of that. Away from them, I mean."

"You know, I haven't lived here since I was ten. And I never can again." I can never live here, where I came from. My sisters are here now, the oldest one and the youngest one and almost all their children and almost all their grandchildren. Our ancestral land, where they were born, but I was not, is their home; it can never be mine. I will remain, as I have long been, estranged from the land I belong to.

"I know, Mom. That's okay, isn't it?"

"This is where . . . the closest thing I ever had to a home. This is where my memories begin." It should be different. But it isn't. "Yes. It's all right. I'm glad I got away from them and out of all that too." It's getting late. Our journey home, our visit, is over. I reach down and touch my father's tombstone for just a moment before we leave, look back one more time. I have so little to pass down to my daughter, it seems. Just the stories, the history, who we came from: we are of the Salish People, the Coeur d'Alene tribe, and this is our country. The first ancestor whose name we know was a man born in about 1820, and his name was Colemannée, which translates as Dust. The name Campbell comes from Colemannée, and the Campbells are the last remaining family of what was once the powerful, but now little remembered, Turtle clan.

I don't even know what it's like to have a place in my own tribal community, though being a part of an intertribal urban Indian community has been an important part of my life in the past. It was all through my daughter's growing-up years.

As we walk back to the car, she asks me where Colemannée and our ancestors who came before him are buried. Is there another, older cemetery?

No. This is it. Colemannée was not a Christian. Before the people converted, they didn't bury their dead in cemeteries. They didn't mark their graves.

It isn't obvious that my daughter (whose father is of Anglo-Saxon descent) is Indian. But Indian blood shows itself, in her high cheekbones and straight, dark hair and in her dark, dark eyes that are so much like my own. My daughter can choose, as I never could, whether or not to be an Indian. She has always considered herself one. She is planning her future career and preparing for it. She wants to work with disturbed children in either a Native American community or a community that includes Native American people. At her age I didn't imagine a career; I just struggled to survive.

Had I been able to choose—if I could have passed for white—I wonder if I would have. Would I have gone far, far away from my beginning . . . let my heart forget all I was reminded of today: my poor, transient childhood, my

mother and sisters, my alcoholic father and what I am connected to through them (and my children, through me): my
homeland and history, my roots.

I drive back to Spokane very fast, cutting right through the
spectacular scenery, thinking of how I'll be here again all
next academic year. Alone and on my own where I began.
It will be good to be here again. I'm not afraid.

We get back to Spokane before dark and eat at a fast-food
restaurant. Then we take in a new film about present-day
Indians: An FBI agent who is a quarter-blood Indian
ashamed of his roots has to go back to the reservation his
father came from to investigate a case. On the rez, he discov-
ers Who He Is and learns to take pride in His People. After
a lot of fancy fights and car chases. It is action-packed and
full of clichés like the Indian policeman who's such a good
tracker and poetic images having to do with visions of spirits,
drums and feathers, shape-shifters and eagles and things.

ABOUT THE AUTHOR

JANET CAMPBELL HALE is a member of the Coeur d'Alene tribe of northern Idaho. She was born in Los Angeles and grew up on the Coeur d'Alene Indian Reservation and on the Yakima Indian Reservation in Washington State. She is married and lives in New York.